PRAISE FOR
TRACKS IN THE WILDERNESS OF DREAMING

"AN INVALUABLE RESOURCE FOR ALL OF US WHO WISH TO UNDERSTAND OUR DREAMS."—*The Recovery Journal*

"Dreaming is indeed a wilderness that should be explored and not tamed. Robert Bosnak has again entered that enchanting territory, and comes back with absorbing stories and intriguing instructions for responding to our own dreams. His book opens the imagination —a first step toward restoring a way of life oriented toward dream."
—Thomas Moore, author of *Care of the Soul* and *Soul Mates*

"A highly revealing and personal work . . . [Bosnak] offers his unique and well-honed theories."—*The Round Table Press*

"THIS IS A WONDERFUL BOOK about how to enter our personal dream landscapes and a parallel introduction into aboriginal Dreamtime. It is a major contribution by a Jungian analyst into practical methods of amplifying the contents of our dreams through noting shifts in our bodily sensations."—Jean Shinoda Bolen, M.D., author of *Crossing to Avalon* and *Goddesses in Everywoman*

"AN EXCITING BOOK! Bosnak's vivid conversations about dreamwork with aboriginal shamans in Australia show that dreams are necessary for the renewal of human life and our relationship to the earth."—Linda Schierse Leonard, author of *The Wounded Woman* and *Creation's Heartbeat*

"A BOOK THAT IS A DREAM AS MUCH AS IT IS ABOUT DREAMS. . . . Bosnak knows how to bring us into dreams like virtually no other writer on the subject."—*Booklist*

TRACKS IN THE WILDERNESS OF DREAMING

Exploring
Interior Landscape Through
Practical Dreamwork

Robert Bosnak

Delta
Trade Paperbacks

A Delta Book
Published by
Dell Publishing
a division of
Bantam Doubleday Dell Publishing Group, Inc.
1540 Broadway
New York, New York 10036

Part of the proceeds of this book are used to support
an Aboriginal effort to create a permanent record
of Dreaming Tracks in Australia.

ISBN: 0-385-31529-5

Reprinted by arrangement with Delacorte Press

Manufactured in the United States of America

Published simultaneously in Canada

May 1997

10 9 8 7 6 5 4 3 2 1

BVG

Dedicated to Arthur Bosnak (1911–1990)

"Maybe you have not properly fulfilled the rituals of burial. Maybe there is still something you should do for the dead."

—Nganyinytja, 1993

"To me it proved to be a piece of my self-analysis, as my reaction to the death of my father, thus to the most significant occurrence, the most poignant loss in the life of a man."

—Sigmund Freud, 1907
Foreword to the second edition of
The Interpretation of Dreams

Contents

Tracks
in the Wilderness
of Dreaming

CHAPTER 1

The Red Center

THAT MONTH, AFTER MY FATHER'S DEATH, I BECAME DRIVEN TO perform a ritual in my office at the end of each week. On the wall behind my chair, over the fireplace—which used to warm the Cambridge, New England, Victorian room years before I moved in to make it my psychoanalytic office in 1977—hangs an unidentifiable tool that used to belong to an ancient woodstove. A thick cast-iron shaft elbows up in aspiration to a circle at the top, while staying solidly connected to a circle at the bottom end below.

After the death of my father I began to touch the bottom circle, cupping it with my left hand at about the height of my head. Then I would close my eyes and see the galaxy. My vision would travel in a spiral along this Milky Way to the center. There I'd see my father's scalp, with his pride of white hair he loved to comb back in a V between bald, glistening skin (though I never thought of my father as bald). It would hover in the center of the galaxy, where the light was most dense. Many tiny stardust dots would become a cloud of white starlight.

Then I would say: "Thank you for all you have given

and for all you have not given. Now take it all back." I'd send off the turmoil and leave for my leisure at home. My rational self grins with imperious superiority at these childish antics, but to this day, three years later, the foolishness continues to ritualize itself at the conclusion of each week.

Ilyatjari the ngankari, an Aboriginal spirit doctor of the Pitjantjatjara people of central Australia who treats body and soul, sits across from me. His dark, shining face, with curious eyes that observe me with intense dispassion, is all business. He knows how far I've traveled—across continents and hemispheres—and what little time I've got. He wants to talk with me. How do I want to use this less than a week? I tell him that I want to discuss dreams with him. This is a formality, since I had written to anthropologist Diana James, who speaks his language, months before this initial trip to the Australian outback, asking her if she knew of an Aboriginal dream doctor willing to meet with a Western dream doctor to discuss our trade. Ilyatjari had agreed.

"Shall I first tell you how I work?" I ask, so he can observe my work. He nods after receiving the translation. He, his wife, and his sister-in-law obviously think it an excellent idea. They sit on the burnt-sienna powder-fine sand, comfortable in their dusty clothes. My clothes are getting there, but they still have some leftover cleanliness of half a world back, where I packed them in my black backpack. I sit on a travel stool, minding my back, although later, in the heat of our conversation, I will move down to sit closer to them. A speckled brown mutt sleeps stretched out behind Ilyatjari.

I randomly choose the last dream I worked with, since

the work is still fresh in my memory. It had been the dream of a young white man, presented at a Melbourne dream practicum (a dreamwork training using live material of participants). While talking, though, I realize his story is about myself as well; the choice has not been random.

"The day before yesterday, this man in his early thirties presented me with a dream I worked on," I begin. The dream involves a car. I know that Ilyatjari travels the red desert in a four-wheel-drive vehicle. We had seen him enter the camp in a cloud of dust, driving the car from the right hand side, as they tend to do down under, grinning at Diana in an impish kind of way.

"This young man is driving a car from the driveway of his powerful house in England. A great Western home. A mansion. He can hear the sound of the pebbles on his driveway. He loves driving the car. It is an open car. Very powerful. Then he gets to the highway and begins to drive full speed. The motor screams. Full throttle. Suddenly, the motor is doing too many rpms (revolutions per minute) and it is beginning to hiccup and stall, leaping forward, then stopping, shaking the car in nauseating commotion. The driver hears the screaming of the motor, until he realizes that there is a woman sitting next to him screeching at the top of her lungs, terrified. The driver is shocked and wakes up, shaken."

Diana concludes her Pitjantjatjara rendition. All three elders nod. The desert around us is silent, contrasting with the speed of the driven.

"That is the dream. Now, here is what I did. I first asked the dreamer to feel the power of the car. He could feel the power deep down in his body, down to his groin, his genitals, and it felt exhilarating and potent. Then I help him feel the motor, screeching along, not able to satisfy his demand for speed and power, overdoing it. He can feel the impact on the body. This is a very typical Western male dream," I add. "That's why so many Western males end up with heart attacks from working too hard. They're driven. The motor is making more rpms than it can take."

As Diana translates I note that they follow me, that they are well aware of the dangers of high-speed Western power culture. Nganyinytja, Ilyatjari's wife, shakes her head in what looks like disapproving disbelief. I assume she doesn't understand why someone would drive himself to death. But maybe she is thinking something entirely different, while I'm just observing my self-critical reflections about my own hard-driving lifestyle.

"Then I ask the dreamer to feel himself into the spirit of the woman. To let the spirit of the screaming, terrified woman enter him. To let himself be overtaken by the spirit of the woman next to him. First he listens and remembers the tone of her voice. Suddenly he can feel the scream tear through him. He actually feels her scream. He's aware of her terror and feels utterly vulnerable in a way that he hadn't experienced before. That feeling of vulnerability he is left with, after he goes through the fear of the woman himself, is essential to his life. It is this fear that makes him push people away. Experiencing the fear deeply may actually reduce it. Avoiding this fear by driving himself ever harder is dangerous. It makes him isolated, distant from people. He is a lonely man. He drives people away.

"Maybe now he can be with a woman without driving her away, maybe now he can have a family." I conclude this brief synopsis of the Melbourne dreamwork, becoming aware of the fact that the importance of family is something universal, which everybody understands. Some of Ilyatjari's grandchildren are making a racket in the background, together with Diana's six-year-old son. I have made the dreamer appear more isolated and terrified than he had actually been in Melbourne, but I wanted to bring out the full potential impact of such a dream.

"That is a good way of working," Ilyatjari relays back to me. I blush. The two women are moved at the thought of this terror-driven young man with speed in his heart to the point of breaking. Their eyes are moist.

"How does he work?" I ask Diana.

Ilyatjari's dark brown face looks like that of the gnomes we used to hear about in childhood fairy tales: deeply worked, serious but with a playful gleam in his eyes as he tells a story to Diana, who will translate his tale section by section. Around us is the rust-colored earth, worn and brittle, as though the world were made of dust. Myriad little flowers shimmer, speaking of the recent rains that made the desert flourish. The trees look like they live off drought, with their parchment skin of dried-out bark that ought to be dead but isn't.

As he transmits his response to Diana, I am suddenly reminded of my dream of the previous night, in which I visited the White House to meet with a very insecure President Clinton. A meeting of the Cabinet was taking place; in back of it there was a rectangular pit from which a dark flock of Jurassic bat-birds flew up, flapping their bony, bright red, wide-span wings—an awesome sight. I asked if they were pterodactyls. A man I know said no. They were archaic birds I had never seen. It seems that in the outback of my white-housed Western mind insecurity arises, fearful of losing its central grip, while archaic existence surges up from the pit.

"At night he becomes an eagle," Diana translates. Ilyatjari has been making motions with his palms pressed together, diving forward in the way one describes a water-ski slalom or a plane in an air show. "He swoops down from above to grab the sleeping person whose illness he is to treat." Ilyatjari follows her words carefully, which convinces me that his English is more than rudimentary. He presses his shoulder blades together as though he were flying along with her words, then flaps his arms with exhilarating freedom. "He takes the sick person on his back and holds him carefully." His shoulders are drawn back to a point where the shoulder blades are almost touching; I realize that he is helping the passenger on his back to hold on better, by squeezing him between his shoulder blades as he flies with great speed.

"Then he flies in a straight line to the Milky Way. He says that his head remains his own and sometimes the sick person will recognize the back of his head afterward. But the patient is not allowed to say which ngankari took him on the eagle flight. The ngankari is allowed to say, but the patient isn't. Then he reaches the place in the Milky Way that is like a hand. There the dead ngankaris are."

Ilyatjari draws a kind of hand in the sand and puts little sticks all around it. He works slowly and deliberately; the intensity of his attention almost makes me see the place he speaks of. The red sand portrays his trip to the center of the Milky Way. A sand painting remains behind, commemorating his nighttime journey.

"Those are the sticks. They fall into the sticks, he and the sick man he carries. The sticks pierce them." I see doctor and patient impaled on beams of age-old healer power. "Then he flies back in a zigzag way, very rough, while at the same time trying not to lose the sick person. If the sick person falls off, he will get sick again."

Ilyatjari interrupts her. His motions are wild, then they stop. It is a long story.

"Ilyatjari said that when one is learning to be a ngankari, one can sometimes drop the patient, because one is inexperienced or overconfident. The ngankari learns a lot from this experience. He must start again from the beginning and learn to fly safely," Diana explains. I'm reminded of a terrible timing error I once made with a patient, irritably bursting out with an insight much too early, long before she was ready to receive it, just because I couldn't hold it to myself any longer. It blew her analysis—and it gave me a valuable lesson in containing my irritation, and in timing. While I think how much more we profit from our mistakes than do our patients, Ilyatjari is explaining something in a more discursive manner, not like the breathtaking flight of a moment ago. I wait for Diana's translation.

"Often the sick person after such a ride wants to become a ngankari, a medicine man, but Ilyatjari will say that he can't. Only after many flights is that possible." I laugh and say that it is the same in analysis. In the beginning of analysis, many people want to become analysts. We call it transference.

"The next morning he sucks out the sticks from the sick person."

That's it. Cured. Who's next!

"Has he always been able to do this?" I ask, hoping my question will not betray my acute pangs of envy.

"He says he always had the second sight. That he could see things others couldn't. But then, when he was in his teens, he lost it because he ate porcupine. That seems to be bad for ngankaris and for the second sight. But then an old ngankari told him that it would come back slowly. And so it did. His eyes opened again and his mouth opened. So he could suck out the bad from the sick."

Ilyatjari's eagle flight reminds me of the flock of archaic red-winged birds I saw last night. The Milky Way is the perfect description of the universe of dream, where the soul travels through a world of shimmer, real as the heavenly bodies.

The ngankari actually flies. He doesn't just think he flies, he *flies*. The experience is as real as my twenty hours of flight to Australia. I flew through the air, and he flies through the essence of space.

From dreams, we know that the *presence* of neither space nor physicality depends on matter. Although the dreamed environment is nonmaterial, it presents itself as physically real. This is one of the few laws of human experience that hold true the world over. *While dreaming we are completely surrounded by apparent physicality.* Several hours every night, archaic birds rise from the pit, oblivious to the laws of day.

With a shock I remember the weekly ritual for which my reason pokes fun at me, when I visit my father in a bright cluster of stars in the galaxy. Half a globe and fifty thousand years of civilization apart, we see the same: he, his dead medicine men in a concentrated hand of the Milky Way; me, my dead father in a dense cluster of galaxy.

That night a dream-cycle with my father begins. I embrace him after finding out that he hasn't died. My father-dream cycle will be flanked by two embraces: one at the outset, one in the end.

Death and renewal is stirring my core. In dreams, buildings topple, earth quakes; my trip to the Center has shaken me.

CHAPTER 2

Act of Genius

I DREAM OF A BEAUTIFUL WOMAN.

When I wake up, I find her in my kitchen. She's an acquaintance who's come for a visit. I blush when I see her. She doesn't. She just smiles politely and continues her conversation with my wife. I know that *she herself* was not in my dream, because otherwise she would blush crimson. So who was her identical dream-counterpart, loving me while I was asleep?

Some people would say she was a wish of mine. And sure, I can't deny that I would love to feel her in my arms as a woman of my dreams. But that doesn't say anything. It doesn't explain who the person was with whom I had a dream romance. While I was actually dreaming, the bed in which I found myself was real, the sheets were clearly sheets; everything felt entirely physical. But who was she who lifted her chemise invitingly, revealing herself to my desire? Her flesh looked and smelled real, felt soft like tender skin. Most of all, not for a moment did I doubt her absolute reality. I knew at that moment that I was with *someone*. With another *person*. Yet she is not, as is apparent a

few minutes (and another world) later, the beautiful acquaintance in my day world. Then who is she?!

I have an answer to this: I don't know.

But not just the kind of "I don't know" like "I don't know
where my socks are" or "I don't know where Timbuktu
really is," but a not-knowing so profound that it makes me
shiver. I *passionately* don't know. Dreams to me are a mystery and so are the inhabitants of the dreamworld.

This absolute not-knowing became apparent to me, ap-
propriately, in a dream. The dream has worked on me ever
since I first took part in it in 1983, forever changing my
basic attitude toward dreaming.

**It is morning. With my son, David, I have been walking
around my alma mater, Leiden University in Holland. We
are walking along the main canal, the Rapenburg, just past
the bend across from the old University Library. It is a nice
day and I'm pleased to be able to show him my old stomping
grounds. We are approaching the bridge next to the Academy, the central building of the university, built in the thir-
teenth century. I point out the most important features of
the town, reminiscing about the good times I used to have
there. My youth is very present to me. My son is about nine
years old during this walk.**

**Suddenly I see something in the canal. I look closer, and
notice it is some kind of ancient statue. I point it out to
David. We look at each other and without hesitation we
both jump in. The water isn't very cold. I dive under and
begin to pull the statue up. It is Mercury, the one of the
winged feet, carrying his staff with the two snakes, his left
hand up in the air in the way you would hail a cab in New
York City. This image adorns the ring I always wear on my
left ring finger.**

We struggle to get the statue out of the water. It is hard work and has a solemn feeling to it, as if we were excavating something ancient and sacred. With great effort we succeed in getting it onto the quay. We stand and look at it. It is at this point that I realize I am dreaming. I look at the bridge and see that it is entirely real. I feel the ground under my feet and know it is firm. I look at the sky and observe the clouds. This world is absolutely real, and yet I know for sure that I am dreaming.

Now David is gone. In the distance, on the same side of the Rapenburg as I am now standing, I see a cab coming toward me. There are no people in the street, but I have to share my excitement with someone: I know that I am dreaming, and yet this world is entirely real. So I rush out into the street and stop the taxi. The cabdriver lowers his window and looks at me, a questioning look on his face. I yell at him, "I'm dreaming. This is all a dream. You are part of my dream!"

At first the cabdriver looks incredulous. Suddenly he seems to realize that I must be some kind of lunatic, and the expression on his face is a combination of boredom and slight disgust. He rolls up the window and drives off.

I would have reacted the same way as the cabdriver. Wouldn't you? If someone told you that you're part of his dream, you'd think that person must be insane. The cabdriver *lives* in the world that I call "dream." At the very moment of the dreaming itself, his existence is as real to him as mine is to me now. The fact that, when awake, I call their world "dream" means nothing to the people who live there. We don't know whether the dream people exist beyond the moment of our presence in the dreamworld, but one thing is apparent: from the perspective of the inhabitants of each particular dream, the reality they find themselves in is *their* reality. Dream people like the taxi driver live inside this reality—this physicality surrounding them everywhere—in the same way that the "I" in the dream lives inside the dreamworld with the unshakable conviction that the surrounding reality is, indeed, utterly real.

If the dreamworlds and their dwellers are real and entirely unknown to us, they must belong to *wilderness*, to unknown lands with laws of their own and creatures untamed, fascinating, and frightening. In psychoanalysis we call these realms "unconscious"—which, of course, means "I don't know," or "I don't know what I'm talking about."

A profound not-knowing is hard to bear. We wake up and try to get a grip on our dreams. We tame them with interpretations. We try to make them into pets, to render them relatively harmless, not like the unpredictable wild creatures they really are. We tell our dreams that they are *our* dreams, that we created them. We tell them they are the random products of the crossfire of synapses, or perhaps the creations of goddesses and gods. We try to convince them that they are metaphors, a subtext of our existence, that they are a reshuffle of unbearable childhood experience. We bind them in weavings of reason, until they are butterflies pinned to the grid of self-knowledge.

Yet, each dream is an act of genius. Ponder this:

A dreamer creates an entirely real world, to the greatest detail. Each dream arouses within us the conviction that we are in our waking lives. This fully awake dream state has precision; it has detail; it has shapes that are likely and sometimes unlikely, yet realistic enough to make us certain as to the status of our consciousness. Compare this with the greatest human-made work of visual art you can imagine. The Sistine chapel in Rome comes to mind. When we look up at the ceiling we are awed by the extraordinary power of Michelangelo's genius. Yet we are not convinced that, if we were up at the ceiling, we could jump into those heavens—something of which a most ordinary dream of jumping up in the air while walking in a field on a sunny day can convince us, with the greatest of certainties.

While dreaming we know that every tree is real, that every particle of air is real into the depth of our lungs; we know that the sky is bright with the light of utter reality. We know a three-dimensional world surrounds us on all sides: a world that is not just above us, as is the ceiling of the Sistine chapel, but *everywhere*. This simple world, created by the dreaming genius, is more real than the greatest work of human art.

Then who is the dreamer?

From the point of view of dreaming we know who he or she is not. The dreamer cannot be the person we call "I" in the dream, since we can immediately observe that the dreamworld is a much wider reality than just that of the "I." Imagine for a moment that you are dreaming. You hear a person say the following sentence: "This entire universe was created by me." Since you are dreaming, you are utterly convinced that you are awake. Apply your waking mind to this sentence. It has a definite ring of megalomania to it, doesn't it? Thus, from the point of view of dreaming, the dreamer is not the "I" in the dream.

There may be several persons besides "I" (such as the cabdriver) acting apparently on the basis of their own consciousness. They appear as though they are in a similar position as "I." They appear equally convinced that they are awake and that they exist in a world. If it is megalomaniacal to assume that "I" is the creator of the world, it holds true for the other people as well.

The dreamer must be a creator of worlds. This dreaming genius—or geniuses—creates world after world during a *full twenty years of our existence* (if we live to be eighty years old), as can be extrapolated from the latest in laboratory-based dream research, conducted in Italy. If this new Italian research is correct, we dream some six hours of every eight-hour night. This mind-boggling fact is the most common human reality. We eat, we breathe, we dream. Just the mere fact that we live in the constant company of this dreaming genius makes dreams of interest. Twenty years of human existence is spent in pure creativity!

Yet, who the dreaming genius is, or who the dreaming geniuses are, I do not know, in the most absolute way I am capable of not-knowing. This not-knowing is a passion, it is like a thunder in my system.

Is the creative dreaming genius *mine?*

The genius created the Leiden University of my youth, the Rapenburg canal, my son and the cabdriver. And, in the same way, this genius created me walking through its creation. I am a particle in the whole of dreaming's creation. The dreaming genius is mine in the same way the world is mine. *My* world, *my* dream, *my* creative dreaming genius: it is mine inasmuch as I belong to it. It does not belong to me. Instinctively I'd say that the genius is—or geniuses are—as it were, dreaming me.

But this is all philosophy. When I speak about the dreamer I am usually in my naive state of mind and use the word to indicate a person who has, or has had, a dream.

What would it take—what would it mean—to enter dreams as mysteries? Would they make us understand ourselves less and less, and open the abyss under our feet, pulling out from under us the clean, well-insured rug of reason?

When first I started working with dreams, the discomfort of not-knowing was alleviated a bit by my illusion that there were people around who actually knew what dreams meant. People who, through years of training, could tell me what dreaming was all about. But as through the years this illusion evaporated, the buffer gone, my discomfort became acute. More so because by then people were actually paying me for knowing something about dreams. Each working day I set out to sell the Brooklyn Bridge to unsuspecting folk who believed that my certificate of Jungian training meant I knew about dreams. At the same time, however, I became aware that the greater my tolerance for knowing nothing about dreams, the more profound were the results of my dreamwork. Like an ignorant fool I had stumbled upon the discomfort of dreaming-as-mystery. Since olden days, initiatory experiences with the ultimate unknown in a ritual setting had been called the mysteries.

The more ignorant I became in the world of dreaming, the less protected I was from the immediacy of dreaming reality. Thus the ritual of dreamwork initiated me into the mysteries of the unknown.

Upon my return from the outback, in Adelaide, I dreamt that I had to give a talk about the Eleusinian mysteries, the widespread initiation rituals in antiquity, during which initiants were confronted with the mysteries of the Underworld.

"What kind of dreams do you remember?" I ask Nganyinytja, a leader of the Pitjantjatjara women who had come to our camp before her husband, Ilyatjari.

We had left Alice Springs the day before, driving for eleven hours along ever smaller roads into Pitjantjatjara land. Diana had taken out the necessary special permits for me and my wife and daughter to travel in Aboriginal land. We had picked up one of our bush guides, Nganyinytja's sister-in-law, a kind woman with a winning grin and remarkably thin legs. She'd been in Alice to care for her husband, who was in the hospital there, and traveled with her grandson, a young boy with a cold and the most curious wisps of flaxen hair around his dark head. He lay quietly on his grandmother's lap as we hobbled along bush roads in the sturdy old vehicle that would have done well in ads for Camel cigarettes. Neither of them spoke English, and since Diana had to keep her eye on the road, we communicated with smiles and expressive exclamations. When we arrived at our campsite it was night. We rolled out our sleeping bags and were completely unprepared for the stars. I had never seen so many stars before: clouds of them with endless depths—sprays of bright presence in a pitch-black universe.

This morning Nganyinytja came into our camp while we were eating the peanut butter sandwiches of Western civilization, and sat down next to the wood fire with its billycan of boiling water, waiting for us to pass her a cup of tea. Diana had greeted her as a matter of course, the way family communicates. And indeed, Diana had been adopted by Nganyinytja's family twenty years ago. After the introductions we were silent for a while. I'd felt stupid, not knowing the protocol for meeting one of my bush teachers. Then she saw six-year-old Christopher, son of Diana, and broke into an infectious smile that easily bridged the gap between us. After a short conversation we felt comfortable, and I believe it was she who brought up the subject of dreams, knowing that I had traveled to the Center of Australia to talk shop.

After thinking for a moment about my question, she replies, "Others remember dreams with dances in them and dreams with songs in them. These are dreams others remember. Now I don't dream."

At first I am taken aback by her distinction between remembered and forgotten dreams. Why do her people just remember dreams with dances and songs in them? It feels so arbitrary to me. In the face of my silence she speaks more Pitjantjatjara to Diana.

"Her husband once saw a new dance and taught it to the people," Diana translates. Nganyinytja is once again underlining the importance of dance and song in dreams, and I am suddenly aware how intensely cultural our respective notions about dreams really are. She believes that a dream is for her people, not for her personally. She tells us of a dream she once had:

We are dancing in a circle. We are inviting all kinds of people to join us. The circle gets larger.

I am immediately reminded of all the work Nganyinytja has done to enlarge the understanding of Aboriginal culture. She has invited people to her land to speak about matters we all hold in common: nature and the land. She has fought her own people's unwillingness to share lore with Europeans (as the white population is referred to). She is one of the outstanding communicators in the Aboriginal community, inviting more and more outsiders into her circle of understanding.

After she tells me the dream, I make an observation about how the dream seems to reflect her daily endeavor

to widen the circle of understanding of the land. Diana
translates my comment.

Nganyinytja looks blank. For about five minutes Diana
tries to explain the idea that the dream may be related to
her private life. In the end Nganyinytja replies with a luke-
warm, "Maybe."

That's as far as we get. To her it is obvious that the
dream belongs to the people, and it is an odd thought
indeed that it might have an interior, personal relevance. I
don't even try to pull out my bag of Jungian tricks, which
would have the dream refer to the increasing sense of self
and wholeness she gains from her circular expansion. Who
cares, anyway? My interpretation would add nothing to
the value the dream holds for her. Apparently, what has
value in her world—like land, for example—belongs to
the community. Dreams are like the land: to her, land
exists in relationship with a people, while to us land belongs to individuals. Thus, to her, dreams worth remembering are those with a collective value, while we look for
individual self-reference in our dreams. We do agree, however, on the fact that dreams are of *some* kind of value.

There is silence again. The old red hills overlook our
camp. Young Christopher is riding his little dirt bike
through the sand. My college-age daughter is still asleep.
I'm relieved when I am asked to get some water from the
huge plastic container that has been driven in here to provide us with tea, coffee, and dishwater. Some mangy dogs
lick up the spills before the water disappears into the rusty
sand. My wife, Deanne, sits with Diana and Nganyinytja
around the fire, talking. I am reminded of Aboriginal
paintings with their U-shapes surrounding dotted circles,
signifying women around a campfire.

That's the moment when Ilyatjari enters the camp in a

cloud of dust. As he gets out of the car I instinctively bow to him in the Japanese way—probably because it is the only truly foreign culture I am familiar with. He looks at me for a moment, then turns to Diana and yells something to her in Pitjantjatjara. They laugh. I grin self-consciously, the kettle in my hand.

After I help him unload some of the dead wood from his truck onto the woodpile, I sneak away to wash the dishes in the plastic pails Diana has filled with hot water. I am glad to feel my hands engaged in relatively familiar activities.

Diana puts everything away in boxes, and switches hats from camp counselor to anthropologist/interpreter. It is then that we have the conversation about Ilyatjari's eagle flight.

Ilyatjari has taken off to do some errands. Nganyinytja and her sister-in-law remain. I don't know if I can keep asking questions, but I'm very eager to hear about the "bush telegraph," the communication Aborigines have with each other, which we Westerners with our superior knowledge know for a fact to be impossible. I had first heard the phrase from Dr. David Tacey, an outstanding and respected Melbourne professor, born in Alice Springs, who grew up with Aborigines. He told me that he once took a year off from his academic training to get some sense of the real world. He decided to pick oranges for a living, and worked side by side with Aboriginal people. Many of them have all but completely lost touch with their tribal background, living on the fringe of the larger Australian cities, cut off from ancestral connections.

One such man was working alongside David, picking oranges. Suddenly he turned to David and said, "My mother has died. When I picked this orange I knew." The man left work that very instant and traveled over a thousand kilometers north to arrive just in time for his mother's funeral. She hadn't been ill.

Without the slightest reason to doubt David's story, I chalked it up to mystery and became very curious about the bush telegraph. In my work I often know things I'm not supposed to know—a receptive faculty I try to train.

Dreamwork creates intimacy to the point of symbiosis. Sometimes in such a close relationship—engendering a great deal of unconscious activity, as dreamwork inevitably does—communication does not seem to be mediated by the senses, as in the case of speech or the observation of gestures. It appears to be a direct, *immediate experience of another's state of mind.* I've come to call this extraordinary mode of transmission *symbiotic communication.* Since this kind of communication is often startling, effecting profound results in dreamwork, I'm trying to understand it better. In going to the outback, my hunch had been that Aboriginal people could provide me with parallels to my own experiences.

While teaching a dream practicum in Sydney, I met a woman who told me that she was once given a grant to do theater with outback Aborigines. She crisscrossed Australia, often not knowing where she would end up next, but she regularly found people waiting for her on the bush path, saying they were expecting her, knowing why she had come. There were no telephones, no travelers preceding her, passing along the news. *She* hadn't anticipated her own arrival at these locations, usually letting chance be her travel guide, so how did they know? After some months, though, she took this behavior for granted, the way the Aborigines seemed to do. This dream-practicum participant didn't invent this story to make herself seem interesting. Her bafflement about it was genuine and profound, even though she had come to accept it as an everyday reality. Another mystery.

Putting my quandaries about bush protocol aside, I ask Nganyinytja point-blank about the "bush telegraph." She is not surprised by my question and begins to explain to us how it works.

"If I get a certain twitch or itch on my nose, I know that soon a stranger will come," she tells me matter-of-factly. Her sister-in-law nods, repeating Nganyinytja's sentence. Nganyinytja continues, as if she were explaining a grammar of some sort. "When I feel something in my hip, I know something important has happened concerning my spouse. Something happening to my aunt or sister is in my upper arm. My thigh has to do with my son or uncle." Her sister-in-law taps the parts of her body that Nganyinytja mentions. "Is this so for all the Pitjantjatjara?" I ask, struck by the ordinariness of her description. They both nod. It is true for everyone. It seems to be a communication system that everyone agrees upon. This is the first time I have actually heard of *a systematic, collective, physical grammar of extrasensory perception.*

They explain that it only seems to work for the immediate family. If something major, usually an accident, happens to a family member, they know through this basic telepathic grammar. As an exchange I offer them a story of my own family.

When my niece was an infant, my brother noticed that whenever my sister-in-law dozed off, their infant daughter, in another part of the house, would begin to cry within fifteen seconds. My brother is a rather levelheaded lawyer, so he observed it carefully. He told me that when they were in bed, every time his wife's head nodded over her book, he would begin to count. For months, the amount of time, about fifteen seconds, never varied, then the crying would begin down the hall.

The two women from another world know exactly what I am talking about.

I am reminded of a study done in yet another world, the Soviet Union of 1967, in which it was observed that "telepathy flashes most often between members of a family, people in love, and childhood friends."* Dr. Pavel Naumov, who conducted his studies in a Moscow gynecological clinic, states that "the biological ties between mother and child are incontestable. In the clinic, mothers are in a distant section, separate from their babies. They cannot possibly hear them. Yet, when her baby cries, a mother exhibits nervousness. Or when an infant is in pain, for instance as a doctor takes a blood specimen, the mother shows signs of anxiety. She has no way of knowing the doctor is at that moment with her child." A two-way hookup is apparently the hallmark of this inborn telepathic connection. A mother is in severe pain. The baby senses it and cries. "We found communication in 65% of our cases," Dr. Naumov concludes.**

In an interview I had conducted just before my arrival in Australia, a respected and reliable native Hawaiian elder, professor Abraham Piianaia, founder of the Hawaiian Studies Program at the University of Hawaii, told me— without any sense of the unusual—that one day when he was small, and was walking with his grandmother, she had

---

* Sheila Ostrander and Lynn Schroeder, *Psychic Discoveries Behind the Iron Curtain,* New York: Bantam, 1970, p. 33.

** *Ibid.,* p. 32.

looked up at a certain cloud formation and said that one of her close relatives had died. And so it was. The next day news came from the other island that this very relative, who had not been ill, had died around the same time his grandmother saw the cloud.

By far the most complete description of this mysterious form of communication comes from one of the great explorers of the twentieth century, Loren McIntyre, who, shortly after 3 P.M. on October 15, 1971, discovered the source of the Amazon river system. This feat was much more arduous than the great expedition of the previous century to the source of the Nile. The Nile was universally thought to be the longest river in the world, until McIntyre's discovery gave primacy to the Amazon: When measured by the southern channel of its delta, the Amazon River is the longest in the world—a fateful shift of focus to the greatest organic wilderness of all.

McIntyre's credentials are completely above reproach, his honesty authenticated.

His story is faithfully recorded by Petru Popescu in the landmark *Amazon Beaming*, a book Popescu wrote with McIntyre. On the jacket of the book we read: "Making first contact with a tribe of Mayoruna, the elusive cat people of the Amazon basin, McIntyre was kidnapped by the tribe and pulled deep into their mysterious and ancient culture. He found himself communicating telepathically with the head shaman. . . ."

This head shaman transmitted complicated "thoughts" to McIntyre, conveying his dramatic plans for the future of his tribe. Only later did McIntyre have access to a translator who spoke Portuguese as well as Matse, the Mayoruna language, virtually unknown outside their tribe. Verbal discussions following these "beamings," as McIntyre calls them, exactly confirmed the content of the messages that had been transmitted nonverbally between shaman and explorer.

After taming his incredulous and dismissive Western scientific mind, McIntyre asked the interpreter about this mysterious transmission. It is called the "old language," he is told simply. Head shamans pass it on through their family line, or through apprentices. The translator only knows about it, but cannot do it himself. Only the "headman" can.

By now I am very excited, and want to convey my own experiences with symbiotic communication in dreamwork.

I want to tell them about the feelings I've experienced, which weren't just mine, while working on others' dreams. Often they represented an atmosphere the dreamer was experiencing as well.

Some moods seem objectively present in the room. Moods appear to be an *environment*, the way dreams are.

For example, a dream experienced with fear may have a frightening *atmosphere*. When such a dream is entered during dreamwork, this atmosphere may be experienced directly by the dreamworker as fearsome. Thus, I take my own feelings and sensations, while listening to the dream recounted, as both my personal responses *and* as a barometer of psychological "weather." The dreamer, by taking me into the dreamscape, exposes me to her climate. My innermost feelings could—possibly—be *her* weather in *my* system. When waking consciousness manages to hover close to the dreamworld, such emotional fusion is, experientially, likely to happen. I understand individuals to be not *just* particles, but also loci of emotional fields that can be received by others in the way a radio receives the airwaves, or like the skin of a chameleon turning into the hues of its environment. This reception can cause disturbances in our own state: thus it is possible to perceive the emotions of others by observing disturbances within. Much of my teaching work consists of training myself and others in honing this perceptive faculty. I sometimes feel like a chameleon carefully studying his own skin.

Interacting with material through *self-observation in a state of symbiosis with the material* is an old art in the history of Western consciousness. It was called alchemy. Not just a precursor of science, it was also a counter force to the ongoing expansion of objective observation that eventually led to the absolute hegemony of science. To the antique art of alchemy, the matter being processed, the laboring alchemist, and the creative imagination that connected them formed one fluid *medium*. Through self-observation the *alchemist participated in* the mystery of his material; the alchemist was a medium by means of which the material represented itself. While working with lead, for example, the alchemist would experience the dark, heavy gloom known as melancholy. Not necessarily the physical result of lead poisoning, this mood was believed to belong to the heavy world of lead he was working on. In the same way, in dreamwork, emotions present in the dream material may emerge in the dreamworker's self-experience.

By way of their collective Pitjantjatjara grammar of physically experienced extrasensory perception, Nganyinytja and her sister-in-law have just given me a prime example of our human capacity to participate immediately in the experience of others. I'm dying to ask more. But, since Ilyatjari isn't around at the moment, I decide to wait.

CHAPTER 3

While Dreaming
and Upon Waking

MY WIFE AND DAUGHTER HAVE GONE OFF FOR A WALK. I'M WRITING notes to myself on my laptop, hoping the batteries will last. Many thoughts I've had about my work untangle easily in the quiet of our camp. The dim gray light of my screen removes me from the wild red landscape.

What follows is a reconstruction of my thinking based upon the brief allusions I wrote to myself with a dimmed screen to save precious electricity—thoughts about moves a dreamworker makes when faced with dream material.

Like a carpenter who doesn't know much about the microbiology of growing trees, we approach our dream craft with the notion that dreams—even the tiniest of snippets—are fully formed living organisms found in nature. These organisms of mysterious origin we use as material for our work. We don't know how they came to be, just that they are. Even though we have identified some brain processes connected to dreaming, these explain dreaming as much as an explanation of the digital technology that reproduces music on my CD player elucidates the music itself.

The primary tool of any dreamworker is memory. No dream can be worked on if it is not properly remembered.

I differentiate between two kinds of dream: fresh dreams and stale dreams. A fresh dream is one that can be remembered as an actual event that took place in dream life; a stale dream is a narrative *about* events without sensory recall of the actual events themselves. For example, a dream in which I hear banging on the door and a voice yelling "Let us in!" is still fresh when I can recall the actual sound of the banging, or of the voice yelling, or the feeling in my heart and upset stomach, or the intensity of the doubt in my mind as to whether I should let the knocker enter or not. If I just remember *that* it happened, I consider the dream event stale. Freshness evaporates rapidly, sometimes instantly. Most dreams lose their freshness after a few days, though some dreams remain fresh for years, even decades. Some dreams just pretend to be stale—kind of like playing possum. When you look at them more closely, they resume their lives as organisms.

This memory distinction has direct implications for dreamwork. At this point we will look at how we work on live material—fresh dreams.

The two basic premises I start with are that *we have absolutely no idea as to the "stuff dreams are made on,"* and that, *while dreaming, dreams are commonly experienced as utterly real waking events* by dreamers the world over. I have personally witnessed many instances of this transcultural rule while doing extensive dreamwork in Europe, America, Asia, and Australia. Therefore, all we can do is take the dream on its own terms, and just observe the phenomena presented by dreaming reality.

Most perspectives we have used since we began con-temporary Western dreamwork in 1900, with Freud's *Inter-pretation of Dreams,* have been external points of view. Even C. G. Jung, who saw dreams as real, as a reality of the soul, expounds on dreaming from the point of view of waking consciousness. Whether we look at dreams as wish fulfillments, representations of archetypes or subpersonali-ties, metaphors, symbols, or the meaningless gibberish of a randomly downloading computer, we judge the dream from the point of view we have *after* waking up. Even one of the most commonly cherished beliefs among dreamworkers, that dreams carry meaning, is an external perspective. In his ancient treatise *The Pythagorean Life,* Iam-blichus writes of the great Greek philosopher: "When someone asked Pythagoras himself what it *signified* that he had dreamt his father, long since dead, was talking to him, Pythagoras replied: 'Nothing; nor does it *signify* anything that you are talking to me now.' "

Whereas external perspectives are relevant, they differ from our actual experience while dreaming. While dream-ing, knowing I am fully awake, I hear the banging on my door and the voice's insistent request to be let in; I do not experience it as an unknown part of self wanting to enter consciousness, or some such notion. I know *someone* wants to enter. An *actual person* with a loud masculine voice. I know I am scared. I can sense the pounding of my heart deep down in my stomach. I experience heartburn. I know that I am breathing fast. I feel that there might be danger. I am concerned that others might wake up. I don't know what will happen if I actually open the door.

Let's start with the fact that *someone* is making all this racket at my door. This *someone,* this actual person outside, is clearly aware of the fact that he wants to enter. My considerations as to whether I shall let him in are equally as real as his insistence that I open the door. While dreaming, it is obvious that I am not the only one with consciousness. This leads to the conclusion that, *while dreaming, there are several simultaneous carriers of consciousness,* even though the events are usually experienced from the point of view of only one of them.

Since the totality of a dreaming event consists of several simultaneously existing points of view, it is important to explore the potential of experiencing the memory of the dream not only from the point of view of the somebody referred to as "I," but also, if possible, from the perspectives of other "somebodies" as well. If I can experience the dream from the standpoint of the one banging on my door, I obtain a much wider experience of the entire dreaming event than when I observe only "my own" feelings. It is as though dreaming consciousness is emitted on several wavelengths simultaneously: on the Leiden cabdriver wavelength the atmosphere in the dreaming is that of a bored confrontation with obvious insanity; on the Robbie Bosnak frequency this atmosphere is of pure elation. Both these atmospheres belong to the dreaming event. One of the purposes of dreamwork is to experience dreaming events through as many facets as possible.

The experience of the many different—often conflicting —dream emotions puts the dreamer's feeling world under pressure, which creates in the dreamer an acute visceral response. This sharp physical awareness may become a catalyst, *accelerating* the psychological transformation processes that are permanently active in the depth of the human soul.

To get to this visceral way of experiencing, it is essential that each emotion be felt through to its accompanying physical sensation. In the dream of the one who wants to enter, I have to feel to the depth of my belly the fear of the Robbie in the room, as well as the insistence on entering in the power of the fist bonking on the door. When feeling both stomach and fist simultaneously, I physically experience both the muscle power of the unknown and the fear of the world beyond my ken. The cringing in my system is the physical response to the clash of these forces. It is a direct physical mode of awareness.

We experience a dream from the point of view of someone else in the dream through a process of identification with that person. However, identification is an involuntary, unconscious process and cannot be willed by the ego. By force of will I can empathize with another, imagine what another is feeling, put myself in someone else's shoes, but full identification cannot be brought about consciously. Identification is something that happens to me. Still, it is possible to create conditions under which identification is likely to occur.

Identification can be brought about by careful observation, by empathy, and by feeling oneself into the bodily posture or motion of another, combined with an attitude of waiting, of not causing something to happen. The process leading to identification with another dream person is necessarily slow. If we try to bring it about quickly, we usually end up with a projection upon the other dream person. Projection—the process of unconsciously seeing elements of self in another person, while being convinced that these elements truly belong to the other—does not just take place in waking life. It happens in dreams as well. Projection holds up an invisible mirror to self and prevents us from truly experiencing the presence of other.

Let me give an example that includes all the elements of

the identification process and differentiates it from the projection of elements of self onto another dream person.

A woman dreams that she shows a photograph of her family to a man she has just met. The event takes place at a bar.

In my Cambridge office the lights are low, and the members of the dream group are very concentrated. In our work the dreamer, herself an experienced dreamworker, first feels her way back into her bottom, to retrieve the sensation of the bar stool, and remembers the quality of the light. As she does this she becomes aware of the man sitting next to her holding the picture. She is sure that he disapproves of her. Her impression of him is as rather haughty, as if he is looking down on her. She feels small and vulnerable. She purposely remains in this feeling for a while, to explore it; later on this feeling will prove to be a projection of her own concerns onto this man, resulting from the fact that she is attracted to him and from her conviction that men she is attracted to cannot possibly like her. This projection onto men constantly reinforces the rut she's in vis-à-vis the opposite sex.

Now she returns to the moment when she hands him the photograph. She is aware of the humming sound of voices in the bar, but the moment of handing the man the photograph feels very private. She vaguely remembers the people in the photograph: members of her family of origin. The picture itself is less clear to her than the slight trembling in her hand as she hands him the picture. The trembling has to do with her interaction with the man, not with the family shown in the photograph.

She continues the observation of her hand. The man has taken the picture with his left hand and holds it along with her. This is the instant she zooms in on, in a slow-motion style, almost to the point of freeze-frame: she feels the trembling in her fingers and observes the way he is holding his end of the picture. His fingers are gentle. He is holding the picture carefully. She attempts to feel into the fingers, noticing how gently he touches the photograph. His fingers are still, compared with the trembling of her own hand. She waits at this point, feeling the relative ease with which he is touching the picture. She is not trying to figure out what the man might be feeling, because in that case she might just experience the feelings she has *about* the man. Instead she waits on the image in careful observation.

Her family is in the mountains, she now notices. It was a happy time. She can almost see everyone smiling. But she remains concentrated on his hand, focusing especially on his thumb and index finger. Her observation has become very precise. It takes all her concentration to keep herself from letting the image move on. The group helps her to keep focused by asking detailed questions. It helps her resist the natural impulse of the imagination to rush forward. This restraint gives her a feeling of swimming against the stream.

Then, suddenly and spontaneously, she can feel his hand from within. A *transit* has taken place: she is now identified with the hand she has been observing. I understand a transit to be a *spontaneous* shift of the location of consciousness from within one dream person to the interiority of another. In this case the transit took place between her and the man. She now feels his interior self the way an actor can feel a character she is portraying from within. She becomes the medium. The character shapes her. Some other essence takes her over while she remains fully aware it is the essence of an other. She becomes the other character while simultaneously knowing she is herself. The interiority she feels remains his. It continues to be his hand; it does not become hers. The sense of otherness remains acute, while at the same time she experiences the hand from within.

His hand feels stable. He is holding the picture with care. Through his arm she can sense into his shoulder; it is more or less relaxed. The care with which he holds the picture is present throughout his entire body. He cares for this picture. The meeting feels important to him, although not in the romantic way she had hoped. He feels a curiosity about her as a person, while at the same time retaining a self-imposed distance. He does not want to get close to this woman at this point, although he feels caring and is enjoying the moment. All these feelings of his become spontaneously apparent to the dreamer, with a ring of authenticity. It does not feel as though she were making this up. She is observing sensations that had been present all along, but outside the sphere of her awareness. She can sense the relaxation in his body, though she is also aware now of a slight tension in his shoulder as he holds back, maintaining his distance.

This is an unfamiliar feeling to the dreamer—this caring with a distance, yet a true caring nonetheless. She remembers the haughtiness she had previously projected onto him. Now, from within his perspective, it feels not like haughtiness but like a slight, carefully maintained sense of distance. This distance is not a reaction to her personally: it is his way of relating to people.

Without losing her simultaneous observer identity, the dreamer is now identified with the man on the bar stool. She feels how he has been hurt in the past and wants to be careful with women. He does not want to encourage the woman who is handing him the picture; he doesn't want to push her away, either. He thinks she is very intense. It does not put him off, but it does make him guarded. He also feels that this bar is not a very private place. He is more aware of the people around them than the woman herself had been.

The dreamer's attention remains hovering inside the sense of the man's body. Then the identification breaks, and she finds herself back in the dimly lit Cambridge room. Members of the dream group open their eyes at the same moment the dreamer does.

By experiencing this masculine reality from within, she may no longer shy away from men, expecting instant rejection from them. At the same time she might understand that the attitude—both in others and in herself—she understands as haughty is really a kind of human interaction that she, in her craving for intensity, is not familiar with: a cool and slightly distant mode of true caring. Becoming familiar with this way of communicating with the world could change her life profoundly.

To practice dreamwork, consciousness has to hover just above sleep. This awareness on the border of sleep may be called *liminal consciousness*, awareness in between waking and sleeping.

One way of entering this liminal state is by reentering the actual memory the dream has left behind in much the same way we entered the dreamworld itself: as an entry into an actual space, containing living action, a space with objects in it, with borders and forms, with creatures in living animation. We bring the dreamworld back to life by remembering anything we can recall from the dreaming.

We close our eyes and focus our attention on any element of the dream we may remember—even if all we remember is the tiniest of slivers. Then we wait, trying to prevent memory from flitting about like a butterfly, onto the next image. (Since Aristotle, the Greek word *psyche*, soul, has also meant "butterfly.") To our surprise, we find that the act of remembering engenders increasingly detailed recall, one object pulling with it the memory of another. We concentrate on details of the space that was the dream and find the fog yielding shapes. These new recollections present themselves spontaneously, as though they were created by the dreaming world that now surrounds us from all sides, dreaming *itself* while we are awake. At times the detailed "recollection" may not have been part of the actual dream; nevertheless it is a product of its atmosphere.

One of the last remaining things remembered, after a dream has fled from memory, is an atmosphere, a mood. Often it is formless, because the specifics have dissolved in oblivion. Even if this is all one remembers, it is possible to work on the dream, by concentrating on the sensations in the body caused by the mood the dream has left behind. These physical sensations will, in turn, create images—not necessarily the dream images that engendered the mood, but new images that befit the atmosphere of the previous dreaming.

The atmosphere of a dream is *atmosphere* in all senses of the word: the mood of a dreamscape, the atmospheric pressure of the dream's interior, and the medium in which all living dream beings exist.

Upon awakening we often feel ourselves experiencing a sudden decompression, as with the well-known sigh: "Thank God, it's only a dream!" We were just in Hell, and now we're in our own marital bed, safe . . . as it were. In

Hell, one is under a considerably higher pressure than in the so-called safety of one's bedroom. We have been chased by sinister forces, escaped at great risk, and suddenly the bed is deliciously warm. Or we may have just partaken of love, and now the bed is cold and empty. The warm love feels different from the cold loneliness. These are two different atmospheres, different kinds of emotional weather. They are experienced as sudden changes of mood upon awakening.

By getting deeper into the details of recollection, the atmosphere of the dream begins to reappear. By paying close attention to our physical sensations, we can get deeper into this atmosphere and the emotions it engenders. Our waking consciousness is now merged with the dream state. In my dream, the woman-who-is-my-acquaintance-in-our-kitchen, who had lifted her chemise in our love's delight, made me tingle with deliciousness: the viscerally felt mood of the dream from the dream-self's point of view. By returning to the quality of the sheets and the fragrance she has left behind, I can reach back into the tingling of a short while ago. The atmosphere of my desire is reawakened: "I want to be with you!"

Now, when the dream atmosphere has reappeared, we try to effect a transit, a crucial move in the dreamwork. At this point we begin to intensively observe the other person in the dream: for instance, this woman-who-is-not-my-acquaintance.

I first feel myself deeply in my dream body. Then I begin to observe, noticing how easily my attention is distracted. Suddenly the two windows behind the woman become clear. The light is a pale blue, as in early springtime or late winter. Soft. Then I see her. She is young. Her body moves as she raises her chemise over her head. I feel an ache in my heart. I concentrate on my heart region and this ache: an ache for her youth, maybe, and the longing to possess her. I see her breasts, larger than those of my acquaintance, and am aware of her red nipples.

I am entirely engulfed in an identification with the dream-self. Now I want to effect a transit, to identify with the dream-other. I observe her motion, the abandon with which she lifts her chemise, the joyousness and love of life in her movements, the stretch along her chest as she suddenly expands in the delight of her physical being. Her chest arches backward, the pectorals stretch; I can feel the sense of release in her as she removes the final cover over her sensuality.

I wait, staying with these observations. While waiting, I keep my attention focused on her. Then, suddenly, the transit takes place, and I am identified with her. Her mood is very different from that of the dream-self. *The dream-self wants to possess her, whereas she herself is entirely self-possessed.*

Both atmospheres, my longing and her joy in being physically alive, belong to this dream of the woman-who-is-not-my-acquaintance. Both have to be *felt* in order to know the dream again: knowing in the biblical sense, with an awareness that fully enters into another.

Finally, there follows an attempt to feel these different atmospheres in rapid succession, to see what happens when they mix. First I feel these moods individually, separated, then I begin to feel them as a mixture of each other. Besides the potential for my male-centered self to experience women differently, this mixture of feelings brings me close to the totality of the dreaming event. The more I approximate the totality of dreaming, the closer I get to my dreaming genius, and thus to one of the creative sources of my being. This shift from the periphery to the core of existence has a transforming effect.

Dreamwork Experiment

In the dream practica I have led over the past fifteen years, we developed an experiment that makes it possible to experience directly what I have described above. This experiment makes it possible to work on live, fresh dreams by ourselves, without any exterior help. You may find, however, that you need some external stimulus to keep you from drifting off. In that case, audiotape the countdown, the count-up, and the other instructions detailed below and play them while you're doing the experiment, stopping the tape whenever you need to linger longer.

Find yourself a spot where you will not be disturbed for half an hour. (For some people, finding such a spot may be an exercise all by itself.) Try this experiment lying on your back, or sitting in a meditative pose on the floor or on a chair; in short, find the most comfortable position that does not hamper your breathing. Slowly read through the instructions below. They are divided into four stages of descent and one stage of resurfacing. During the descent, we try to get to a liminal state of consciousness in which we almost fall asleep but just barely don't.

When you have understood the nature of the instructions, close your eyes and begin the experiment. It doesn't have to take more than a few minutes, but it can go on as long as you like and as often as you like. For this experiment, choose a fresh dream you can still remember clearly. Recent dreams are usually most suited for this purpose.

This is the program in short:

First, lead yourself down an imagined incline or staircase. Repeat this.

Second, begin at the top of your head, and feel your consciousness sink from your head down to your feet, noticing all experiences on the way.

Third, enter the dream from the standpoint of the dream-self and become aware of your surroundings.

Fourth, observe another person in the dream. Through careful observation begin to empathize, effecting a transit to this other's point of view. Repeat this with various dream-others. Once you are strongly identified with a dream-other, see if you can locate and observe dream-self.

Fifth, once you feel you've had enough, count slowly from one up to twenty, noticing how consciousness decompresses as it moves back up to the surface.

To choose an appropriate dream, do a short preliminary test: look around you and observe the space you are presently in while reading this book. Observe objects around you and concentrate on a few. See how the light hits them. Notice the distance between yourself and the objects you have focused on. Realize that you are *in a space* that surrounds you on all sides. Then close your eyes and try to remember the space you've just observed and the objects you've focused your attention on. Spend a few moments doing this. Then shift your attention to the dream you have initially chosen for this experiment. If you can remember *any* part of the dream as clearly as you remembered the space you are presently in, it is a good dream to use. Even if there is only a single scene you can still remember spatially, take that scene to experiment with. If, however, the dream feels more like a story than a spatial event, you'd better choose another dream.

The dream image you select for this work should be one in which there is another dream person: a human, an animal, or any other kind of presence. One of the objects of the experiment is to move the location of consciousness away from the dream-self into the other person, in order to experience the dreaming from the point of view of a person other than self.

Step 1

For an initial induction into liminal consciousness—an awareness floating between waking and sleeping—become aware of your breathing, and then begin to count from twenty down to ten. With each number, imagine taking a step down stairs or down an incline. As you go down, feel how you sink deeper and deeper toward sleep. When you reach ten, stop for a moment: feel what state of consciousness you're currently in, and think about whether it feels different from the moment when you started to count. (It doesn't matter whether you feel different or not at this point. *Wondering* about it is what matters here, since it may make you aware of the possibility that your state of consciousness *can* shift.) Then count down from ten to zero, all the while sinking down deeper still.

You will come very close to the place where you fall asleep. You have to try to stay just above sleep, reaching a level where you are as close to being asleep as you can be without dozing off. It demands effort, like walking a tightrope: if you fall off, you drift off to sleep.

Step 2

When you have reached this liminal state between waking and sleeping, count down again from ten to zero. This time, while counting, focus your consciousness first in the very top of your head, then let the focus of your attention sink slowly down, through your head and neck, through your whole torso and arms, through your genitals, down your legs, down to your feet. When your attention is focused in your feet, enter the dream image you have chosen.

Step 3

Now position yourself in the same dream place where the dream-self was located, and start looking around.

Is it light in the space, or dark? What is the light like, bright or dim? When you look ahead of you, what do you see? What do you become aware of when you look ahead? Are there any objects you can see? Turn slowly to the left. What do you become aware of? Is this a large space that you are in? Is it a high space, or low? Focus on one object and estimate how far away you are from that object. What is the shape of the object? What is its texture? How does the light hit it? Turn some more, to whichever side you want, and begin to observe as many objects as you can— but turn very slowly, very slowly. You try to go as slowly as possible. Each time you notice an interesting object, observe it carefully and try to estimate the distance between you and that object. Become aware that you are surrounded on all sides by an environment.

Are there any sounds? Are there smells? What is the ground like under you? What is the ambience of the space you are in? Is the atmosphere tense or relaxed, bright or

dark, pleasant or unpleasant, depressed, elated, or somewhere in between?

Step 4

Look around the space and locate any other being in
the space with you. For purposes of identification I will
call that person "other" and call you "self." How far away is
self from other? Estimate the approximate distance. What
does self feel about other? Does self like or dislike other?
Concentrate. Feel throughout your body what self feels
about other. Observe other. What do you expect other to
feel? Make a mental note of this. (This is in order to compare, later, the inner world of self—its expectations and
projections—with the actual experience of the interiority
of other.)

What kind of body position is other in? What kind of
posture? Is the posture of other tense or relaxed? Eager or
detached? If other is moving, notice the movements of
other with a choreographer's eye. Now feel in your body
this posture or these movements. How does it feel to be in
such a posture or in such motion? Just feel it. Use your
body to mimic the movements or the posture. What does
it feel like to mimic these movements or this posture? (If
possible, do all of this without actual movement. Just feel
yourself deeply into your sense of body.) Observe other
carefully while you do this. See if you can feel the body of
other from within. Now wait, while observing carefully,
using your entire body to help you observe and empathize. If there is any part of the body of other you can
feel more closely from within, concentrate there.

If self and other are looking at one another, focus on
this look. What do you see in the eyes of other? What is

this look of other conveying to self? Is there a mood in this look? Wait and observe.

Another good place for focusing attention is on the backbone of other. Feel it with your backbone. What does the back of other feel like? *Good points of entry into other are through sensing eyes, a look passing between self and other, posture, backbone, or motion.* Now wait until you feel other from within.

Suddenly it will feel easy and natural to feel other from within. *Wait* for this moment. This is the identification you are after. It may take some time. *Hover* around this point of concentration. The transit takes place almost unnoticed: you will find that you can easily feel from within other. How does other feel? What is other feeling physically?

Now begin to observe the space from other's point of view, from other's position. Just look around. How does other see the space? Is it dark or light for other? Is it a large space? Other may experience the surrounding environment differently than self.

Now other locates self, and begins to look at self. What does self look like from point of view of other? Just look at self and observe.

As other keeps on observing self, and looks around the space, what is the atmosphere? Are there sounds other hears? What else is other experiencing? What does other's body feel like now? What is other's posture or motion like now? Feel the posture or motion of other from within. Now observe self again.

Stay with this for as long as you can. Keep close to the experience of other. If there are more others in the space, you may want to try and transit into an identification with them. Keep going very *slowly*. Always wait until the empathy passes almost imperceptibly into full-scale identification before you proceed.

Step 5

When you feel tired, or sense you've done enough, or begin to lose the image you've been working on, count up from one to twenty. Don't forget to observe the change in density of your concentration and the shifts of atmosphere as you move back up to waking consciousness.

At first this experiment may give you trouble. The transit to the other is often hard to obtain. It will feel as if you are inventing all this. The voice of reason speaks with certainty that you're involved with the fictitious. But once the recalled dream event becomes again an *actual environment*, the sense of authenticity will silence—for a moment—this voice of reason. Try a few potential transits into other inhabitants of the dreaming, and you will find that suddenly you *can* feel the dream from the perspective of another. Once you have felt this, future experiments will be easier. The more you do it, the less strenuous it will become to hold on to your focus and keep the ambient image stable. As you train your careful attention, the natural tendency of images to flicker and evaporate will diminish, and transits will take place more rapidly.

In case you have the feeling you can't get out of the identification with other after the dreamwork terminates, don't panic. It will slowly dissolve and you'll transit back to your habitual self. Being-self is a kind of habit, like smoking. It is hard to stop smoking and easy to start again. In the same way it is hard to leave the habitual perspective of self, and easy to slip back in.

One helpful way of moving out of a state of panic is by breathing deeply. Let your breath go down as deep as possible into your body. Imagine your breath connecting with your feet. Then notice how your feet are planted firmly on the ground. Keep telling yourself to breathe deeply.

The experiment described above is an effective way of working with fresh dreams on your own. Keep a log to write down your experiences. Keep track of your difficulties with transits and note down which methods of effecting them work best for you. For example, in my case the easiest way of effecting a transit is through careful observation of body posture. I write down in what order it was possible to transit to other perspectives, what was difficult and what was easy. I remind myself how each perspective differed and what associations emerged while working on these interiorities. Whenever I remember a moment in my life when I behaved exactly the way the dream person I've just transited into might have, I make careful note of it. In that way I connect the dream people to my daily life. For example, in Dream 8 in the Appendix, a dream I had in Sydney, my dreamwork leads me to transit into my Viennese psychiatrist friend who has suddenly discovered that what he'd always been looking for had forever been staring him in the face, right across the street from him. I can feel his thin, strong body with its slightly awkward stoop and feel his longing for what he can't have. I am reminded of the way I often can't find things that are right in front of my face because I assume that I won't be able to find them, occupied as I am with far-flung matters. This sometimes gives me the look of a distracted professor. If I wore glasses I'd search for them constantly, though they'd be on my forehead.

If I have the energy, I conclude my dreamwork log report with a description of the entire dreamwork as if it were a dream, remembering as many details as I can. (Since these detailed dreamwork log entries require some modicum of discipline, of which I have precious little, such detailed reports from me are sporadic. I usually have trouble enough doing the actual dreamwork. There are so many reasons not to! Movie rentals, for one.)

If you combine this experiment with the work on dream series presented in Chapter Eight you may be able to work, with some discipline, your own dreams by yourself.

A dream series consists of a group of dreams placed in chronology. The work on dream series has the dreamworker search for interconnections in the vast amount of material presented in the texts of remembered dreams. As an example, in Chapter Eight I have subjected a series of my own dreams—while in Australia—to the rigorous tracking of interlinking paths, creating some kind of map of this particular wilderness.

The more our lives move off the beaten track, the fewer road signs we will encounter. Finally, we end up in the very bush of our lives, a place where we have to navigate purely on an inner sense of direction as we daily are confronted with new terrain. Dreamwork trains us in developing a sense of direction in the absolute unknown. My Australian dream series demonstrates how this inner sense of direction, this homing device, emerged in my life.

I first started to develop my method of working—as demonstrated by the above dreamwork experiment—on the basis of my lucid dream, when I stopped the cabdriver near the Leiden Academy. (A lucid dream is a dreaming event during which one is aware of the fact that one is dreaming.) It became obvious to me that, from a purely phenomenological perspective, the cabdriver was a living being to whom *I* was some kind of lunatic. From where he was sitting, he was living in an entirely real world, obviously not created by the madman who claimed it was his dream. The more I was able to enter into his perspective, the more real his world became. Was I going crazy, losing the distinction between reality and fantasy?

I really would have felt like the lunatic the cabdriver saw me as, had my attitude not been prepared ten years before, in 1973, by another dream in which I just dove in. I discussed this dream with a man I greatly admired, Henry Corbin, the great scholar of Sufism.

In the dream I found myself walking along a river. On the other side of the river I saw a Middle Eastern city of white stucco cupolas. Without hesitation I jumped into the river and swam across. When I walked through the white city I was almost overwhelmed by the reality of the place. It felt more real than anything I'd ever seen before.

I told Corbin this dream because, within weeks of having it, I heard him speak about the City of Light at Eranos, a conference center in Ascona, Switzerland, where, since 1933, various great scholars have tried out their most ground breaking ideas before presenting them to a wider audience. His description of the City sounded so much like the one in my dream that I decided to ask him about it. I was at the beginning of my life, in my mid-twenties, and he was at the end of his, in his mid-seventies. For some reason he was fond of me and turned his hearing aid on while listening to me. Hearing tired him. He lived in a world in which, he used to say with irony, most of his contemporaries had been dead for a thousand years. I loved him. After hearing the dream, he smiled. "You were there," he said. "You were actually there. You were in that

City. That's why it felt so real. You were there because the City exists."

The place where the City exists had been described by him in many of his books, most notably in *Creative Imagination in the Sufism of Ibn-Arabi.* He had called this location the *mundus imaginalis*, the imaginal world. This imaginal world was a state of reality, a realm with an architecture of space and time as real as the world of physical matter, and as real as the world of spirit, metaphysics, pure thought. There were considered to be three worlds: the world of matter below, the world of spirit above, and the world of image in between—each realm entirely real. In the twelfth century, according to Corbin, the middle realm dropped out of Western consciousness, leaving us with the dichotomy of matter and spirit, and eventually with just the science of matter. But when vision was still strong in Europe there had existed an upper world of spirit/mind, a lower world of matter, and an intermediate world of image. While fully awake, visionaries had free access to this latter realm. Their visions were not considered to be their private fantasies, they were understood as travels through a true world, much like the eagle flight of Ilyatjari. Corbin referred to these travelers, following the greatest of medieval Sufi visionaries, Ibn-Arabi, as Knights of the Invisible.

Today I see the prototype of this intermediate realm in the world of dreaming. While dreaming, the imaginal world is objectively *present:* we actually find ourselves there. It is a continuum of space-time, like the material world, populated with bodies that have density and are composed of a substance that is, most likely, nonmaterial.

So, when I met the cabdriver, I was philosophically prepared to return to Western consciousness as it was *before* the twelfth century and consider his existence as real, though *neither material nor metaphysical.* The substance of his existence is something different—*imaginal*—fundamentally unknown, yet real. For the most part, I do *not* consider him to be a momentary embodiment of a permanent other-worldly essence, a spirit in the metaphysical sense. All I know about him is that he exists while dreaming and that he is embodied. Where was he before the dreaming and where will he be after it? I know as little about this as I do about my own being before and after my life.

To my surprise, the therapeutic implications of the method of identification with other dream people *as others* were profound. As a therapist employing dreamwork in order to reach the depths of my patients' souls, to help facilitate modest transformations, this was an exciting discovery. It gave me a way of reaching deeper than I ever had before. It was also a decisive step in my emancipation from my psychoanalytic ancestors—like Ilyatjari's dead ngankaris at the center of the Milky Way—the authorities who reared me in my profession, whose thoughts had made my thinking possible. I had stumbled upon an insight specific to *my* work. Now that I'd authored a thought of my own (inasmuch as thoughts can ever be original to begin with), my relationship to the fathers, Freud and Jung, began to change. The dreams I had while in Australia show a recent installment of this shift in relation to the fathers.

I rigorously stuck with the cabdriver's perspective. Namely that he was *himself* and not a part of me. He was not mine. He was not a so-called subpersonality. I did not own him. He insisted on maintaining his autonomy and dignity. But I could get to *know him from within* through the process of identification I have just described. It turned out to be easier to identify with dream people than with physical day-world people. This may be because a common life force animates both self and others in the dreamworld, since possibly all dream people, including dream-self, participate in the creative life of an unknown superordinate dreaming genius. Most paradoxically of all, though, because the feelings I experienced in identification were not mine to begin with, I could feel them down to a visceral depth much greater than what I could achieve by considering the dream person's feelings as my own—if I had, as has been said, "owned" these feelings. (At this time, owning feelings was all the rage in psychology, and any method of not owning was moving against the tide.) It removed the onus of responsibility for the emerging desires and feelings entirely, since they were not mine, so I could not get mired in traps of guilt and shame accompanying the sometimes horrendous emotions and ugly desires making up the inner life. I was free to feel fully, without blame. Yet, upon such a full experience of interiority, I was stirred deeply and affected profoundly by the feelings that had entered my awareness.

At the same 1973 Eranos conference where Henry Corbin spoke about the City of Light, James Hillman delivered a watershed lecture called "The Dream and the Underworld" (which later appeared as a book of the same title). With this talk Hillman reversed the direction of dreamwork.

Hillman observed that ever since Freud, dreamworkers had gone to the dream to mine it for *meaning* that could be *brought back* to the day world. Freud had said, "Where id was, ego shall be," indicating that the denizens of the land of dreaming should be conquered by waking consciousness, pulled up to the "surface" by their hair, as with the

prototypical caveman's "chivalry" toward women—or like
the colonizer with his thirst to exploit the raw materials of
the lands he conquers. The dream was to be milked for
insights and discarded like an empty old bag in order that
we in the waking life might be the wiser. Hillman proposed a change of direction: to have waking day life feed
the dreaming. My understanding of this was that we
should try changing our exclusively *export*-oriented
dreamwork toward more of an *import* orientation.

Mining dreams for insights about our daily life, our past,
and our problems is the usual way dreams have been
treated. We directly apply what we learn from our work
on a dream to our waking existence. The woman who lifts
her chemise is my feminine side, needing more attention;
my life has to be lived more sensuously. The people who
knock on my door are parts of my dark shadow, elements
of my own masculinity that frighten me; I'd better let
them in, to fulfill my manhood in a more satisfactory way.
The woman on the bar stool has to learn to care for others
without getting so immediately, deeply involved that it
throws her life out of kilter. The insecurity of the president in his White House with archaic pit-birds in the
background means that *my* insecure Western consciousness
has to learn to adapt to a more primitive realm within. Et
cetera, et cetera. By gaining understanding from the
dream, our day life may be affected directly. The direct
therapeutic possibilities are obvious. In the case of my
White House dream I may trace my insecurities to the
earliest, archaic moments of my life, when the feelings of
inferiority reigning in my mother's family shaped my self-
image. I would come to understand myself better, which is
valuable.

All these are "exports" from the dreamworld into daily

life. If in a dream we feel utterly isolated, we therefore must go back to a place in our youth to see how this isolation came about. . . . But wait a minute.

Let's use this isolation example to talk about *imports*:

A middle-aged man dreams that he is sitting by a refrigerator. He feels lonely and rejected. His wife has left. The refrigerator is empty.

In the same way I have shown in the exercise, this man and I return to the dream kitchen. He first experiences the isolation as an icy feeling at the pit of his stomach, and as a sense of emptiness. Through a dreamwork transit, he comes to identify with the refrigerator—and remembers his "icy" mother. He then recalls the moment when his mother left home to go back to school in another city and realizes that, since his wife will go back to school now that the kids have left, he is afraid of being left once again.

At this point we can make all the export moves, understanding and feeling how his wife's impending course of action makes him repeat what he has lived before. This would certainly be appropriate. However, we could also *import* the feelings that came up on the day his mother turned to him and simply said: "I'll be leaving." We can bring them back to the dreaming, to the feeling of icy isolation, sitting next to the empty refrigerator. As we make this importing move, the feelings in the dream are magnified: he suddenly feels himself in a deep freeze. A spontaneous transit has taken place to the interior, frigid core of the freezer. The deep freeze pervades his entire body. He begins to feel a drugged glow of well-being (the point when cold leads to sensations of warmth) as if he were dying of hypothermia, the way mountain climbers who have been saved just in time report the experience of almost freezing to death. He has moved to the core of cold. The feeling of isolation has been essentialized— transformed into a concentrated emotional substance through distillation—by importing a memory from daily life. The dreamer knows the *essence* of coldness.

Suddenly less terrified of the cold feelings of loneliness, the dreamer begins to reflect on the solitary aspects of life. Over time, ice-cold loneliness turns—in part—into a solitary sense of self, an ability to be alone, away from maternal warmth. He clings less to his wife; she feels she can breathe more freely. A ripple effect goes through their entire life; their waking world transforms. Every time he clings to his wife out of his fear of the cold he can return, through dreamwork, to the essence of coldness and wait there until his dread subsides. This is homeopathic therapy: like cures like. He has learned to remedy his dread of coldness with the essence of ice.

The purpose of this example is to show that, *if we let the day world serve the night world*, experiences may come about that feel so intensely real and essential that they directly affect the quality of our vitality, thereby changing dreamers in a fundamental way. It is as though importing feelings from our day life makes dreamwork into a still where, as with alcohol, raw emotion is distilled into a strong spirit. Raw coldness and isolation turn into the pure spirit of loneliness. The experience of the ice-cold pure spirit of loneliness leads to a capacity for being alone. Brewing a core essence from raw emotional material transforms the brewer.

Dreamwork demonstrates that at the core of a feeling which haunts us most, an agent of change may be found that transforms our daytime problems indirectly and profoundly, since it brings about a change in attitude and a different sense of being alive.

So far I have concentrated on the viewpoints that attempt to reenter the state of mind we were in while dreaming, the so-called *dreaming perspectives*.

But then we wake up.

When we are awake and look back at the dreaming as an event in the past, other views emerge, the so-called *waking perspectives*. Waking perspectives run a wide gamut of possibilities.

Of course, the easiest perspective to address is the rationalistic one that considers dreams as meaningless hogwash, soapy bubbles used for brain cleaning. But since this perspective denies any possibility for dreamwork, I merely mention it. If, however, we believe like Jung that psychological laws are by nature paradoxical, dreams are simultaneously meaningless as well as meaningful. Dreamwork focuses on dreams in their meaningful aspect.

The first meaningful perspective we encounter I'll call the *naive* perspective. (I use the word *naive* here without judgment, in the way one talks about naive painting.) Referring back to my dream with my son at the Leiden Academy, this naive perspective automatically assumes that the son I walk around with in Leiden represents my actual son, David. This perspective says in the morning: "Hey, David, I had a dream about you."

The interpretation of the dream from this perspective Jung calls the *object level*, because it assumes that the dream figure refers to its object, its waking counterpart. Jung insists that it is an essential way of looking at dreams when one is in a close relationship with the person one dreams of, since it might refer to an as-yet unconscious perception of her or him.

In this case I indeed *am* in a very intimate relationship with the dream figure. Maybe this dream connotes an unconscious realization that my son and I share the same investigative curiosity and the same mercurial capacities, and that I'd better teach him his way around in this academic world of curiosity and constant change. It may also refer to a need for increased communication between us. Mercury is, after all, the god of communication (as well as of exchange, travel, conniving thievery, and of dreamworkers who guide people to the underworld of being).

On this object level the dream-self refers directly to the waking-self: I in the dream am the same person I am while awake.

Next is the *personality* perspective. After I've told my son I had a dream about him, I may realize that, since all elements presented in a dream are part of the whole dream, each element in the dream must be part of the dreamer. Therefore each element of the dream must be part of the dreamer's personality. David in Leiden is a subpersonality of my dreaming self. He refers to my inner boy who follows his father and learns from him by doing what he does: the part of me that follows paternal authority with complete trust, jumping in at the first suggestion by the father. When I am in my little-boy-David-who-jumps-in-at-the-first-prompting aspect, I am easily enthused, can be gullible toward authority, am starry-eyed, and innocently embrace the cunning of others. Mercury is, after all, the trickster god. Mercury in this context may create an almost innocent delight in lying and cheating, in being a con man who tricks others with abandon—or a childlike desire to communicate and bring people together. (This element of my personality must certainly come to the surface if I am to tame the unethical side of its intentions.) Jung calls this perspective, according to which each element of the dream represents parts of the subject (or dreamer), the *subject level* interpretation.

On the subject level, I in the dream am the part of my personality that habitually identifies being a father with a nostalgia for youth.

What is the relationship between the perspective while dreaming—that my son is a being in his own right—and the waking, subject-level interpretation that sees him as part of my subjective personality? Of course I have no idea, but I can't help speculating on this wave/particle phenomenon in dreaming. (According to quantum mechanics, a ray of light, paradoxically, behaves like both a wave and a particle, depending on the way the observer studies light.)

The persons populating my dreamworld appear to share a common life force with me, the creative life of what I called dreaming genius. It is as though the dream people and I belong to a community of soul that draws the energy by which it is animated from the same vital source. As a result, when I have entered the emotional world of a dream person through identification, I am experiencing a part of this shared life force—a part of my dreaming vitality I am unaware of because it is experienced as other. Thus a dream person appears to be at the same time an independent agent as well as a quality of my own vitality.

Father Teilhard de Chardin describes this beautifully in his book *The Divine Milieu:*

I took the lamp and, leaving the zone of everyday occupa-
tions and relationships where everything seems clear, I went
down into my inmost self, to the deep abyss whence I feel
dimly that my power of action emanates. But as I moved
further and further away from the conventional certainties
by which social life is superficially illuminated, I became
aware that I was losing contact with myself. At each step of
the descent a new person was disclosed within me of whose
name I was no longer sure, and who no longer obeyed me.
And when I had to stop my exploration because the path
faded from beneath my steps, I found a bottomless abyss at
my feet, and out of it came—arising I know not from where
—the current which I dare to call *my* life.

The conclusion appears to be that the dream people, for
whatever reason, are entirely actual and independent
agents, while being at the same time qualities of mine that
can be accessed by way of identification with these actual
others.

Another perspective, one of the oldest, is the *symbolic*. It
sees the images in dreams as referents to another world,
which is absolutely inexpressible yet can be perceived by
means of these symbols. A symbol points to *a reality beyond*
its mere appearance. The symbolic worlds expressed in
religion, art, and literature refer to the metaphysical, the
invisible. A symbol evokes the spirit of its invisible counterpart. A symbol connects the reality of images and forms
with the transcendent, imageless realm of pure contempla-
tion (sometimes described as "not here, not there") called
the world of spirit.

In the Leiden Academy dream, the statue of Mercury is
coming to the surface. (Remember, during the dream it
was an actual statue. The symbolic is a waking perspec-

tive.) Seen as a symbol, the god Mercury refers to the spirit of communication in a world where movement reigns supreme, a spirit of travel and imagination where constant motion matters, a cabdriver's existence, moving people around the map of human endeavor. Mercury rules over quixotic change, deceptive exchange, and radical amorality. (Not immorality, since this indicates a negative caring for morality. Morality just doesn't matter to the mercurial world.) His only absolute: Keep moving.

The spirit of Mercury is that of a shape-shifting transformer, the patron spirit of businessmen, travelers, and thieves, and of those who traffic with the unknown, like dreamworkers, explorers, and spies. According to the medieval alchemists—whose patron Mercury was (incarnate as Hermes Trismegistus) and who were passionately interested in the healing process—Mercury rules over both poison and remedy in healing. As we saw in the work with the man next to the refrigerator, what poisons him, his dread of the cold, may be cured by an immersion in the essence of coldness. From the point of view of the healing arts, alchemy concerned itself with the extraction of medicine from poison.

The Leiden Academy dream symbolizes an initiation into the rites of Mercury. The initiation consists of raising the statue to the surface, then becoming lucid—being fully aware that I'm dreaming while staying firmly inside the reality of dreaming—while both the statue and my son disappear, followed by the confrontation with the cabdriver, symbolizing Mercury in his manifestation as the Traveler. Mercury, the spirit of motion and transformation, changes me from a being-with-my-youth into a man alone, overwhelmingly certain of the reality of the dreaming. This mercurial insight both poisons and remedies my mind: it drives me crazy with the inflated certainty that I have had a major original insight, and it heals me by reducing me to one of the actors in the creative life of a superordinate being.

The *metaphoric* perspective differs from the symbolic. It is the poetic viewpoint, perceiving images as figures of speech. The image of Mercury *coming to the surface* can easily be crafted into metaphor, into a figure of speech. One can viscerally sense the meaning of a process imagined as something rising up, bubbling up, surfacing. Metaphor reverberates with a depth *within* the image. We do not need exterior knowledge to sense its significance. We don't have to go to a symbol dictionary or search libraries of ancient texts. All we need is a poetic eye to unveil the metaphor's heart. A poetic capacity for crafting metaphor from images is essential for dreamwork, as is a wide knowledge of the world of symbols.

There's a stirring in the camp. Ilyatjari is shipping in a truckload of screaming little children. They're more of his grandchildren, I am told. I'm glad he's back. I was just beginning to get tired of writing little didactic notes to myself in telegraph style, while waiting for our next conversation.

My laptop quacks wistfully, starving for juice.

CHAPTER 4

Symbiotic Communication

ILYATJARI HAS HIS BENT LEGS SET TO THE LEFT, UNDER HIS BODY, AS he waits relaxedly for the question I have come here to ask him. I want to talk about *symbiotic communication*, about feeling the emotions and sensations of others by means of direct *participation*.

The notion that such communication, apparently not mediated by the senses, can exist at all does not sit well with our Cartesian world, in which we maintain with certainty that one can feel only one's own feelings and not those of others. This modernistic view sees individuals as particular, as particles filled with content all and exclusively their own, each in a private world that can be shared—at will—through the use of tools of communication.

In dreamwork the participants are not just particles, they are emotional fields as well. It is possible for the dreamworker to fuse with the emotional field generated by the dreamer. Like a dream, *a mood is an emotional ambience surrounding us from all sides.* When we say that there is a certain mood hanging in the room, we mean just that—

that the entire space is pervaded by a particular emotional atmosphere.

Yet we have seen that a dream contains not just one single mood. Dream events may be accessed through a variety of emotional perspectives. The dreaming may be experienced through the emotions of the dream-self (the "I" in the dream) or through the eyes of another in the dream. The experience of Robbie Bosnak running up to a taxi in Leiden is a completely different one from that of the mildly exasperated cabdriver. The former is in the throes of ecstacy, while the latter is annoyed and bored.

In the same way, some feelings a dreamworker experiences through symbiotic reception are not those of the dream-self, but of a dream-other. Sometimes the others in our own dreams carry moods and emotions inaccessible to us. In that case, if the dreamer is enabled by the dreamworker to identify with this dream-other, the emotion disappears in the dreamworker . . . and is experienced by the dreamer. Since it is one of the objectives of the dreamworker's craft to help the dreamer become aware of hitherto unknown elements of existence, the dreamworker takes her own experiences as *potential* experiences of the dreamer. This does not mean, of course, that everything I experience necessarily belongs to the dreaming ambience re-created by the presentation of a dream. *Many* of my feelings and sensations probably belong entirely to *my own subjectivity* and are not the result of an unconscious fusion with an objective ambient atmosphere of the dreamer's creation. Yet sometimes, I have observed, seemingly subjective sensations are the result of an unconscious identification of the dreamworker with elements of the dream. Therefore I consider *all* of the sensations I experience while listening to a dream as *potentially* related to an ambient dreaming atmosphere.

It seems that experiences which are *repressed* by the dreamer can, especially, be "taken in" by the dreamworker. I always imagine it as similar to the law of communicating vessels that was demonstrated to us in high school, with a double container consisting of two test tubes or beakers connected by a thin glass pipe: if the water is pushed down in one, it would rise in the other. Similarly, if a dreamer presses an emotion down, it just may rise up within the dreamworker. Sensations I experience as a dreamworker *may* give me information as to where in the dream to look for repressed emotion. Since the beginning of Western therapeutic dreamwork in 1900, we have looked to dreams for help in accessing emotional realities hidden from ourselves. The trouble with the hidden is that it is hard to find. We cannot, without peril to the whole enterprise of dreamwork, overlook anything that might serve as an indication of the unconscious undercurrents of dreaming.

We dreamworkers have to investigate, always, whether feelings *we* sense are actually present among any of the different points of view existing in the dream. And we have to be careful to do this without imposing the feelings we experience on the dreamer, since a mood thus engendered by us may *not* belong to the dreamer's world, but to ours. One never *really* knows that a feeling or sensation one experiences as a dreamworker has anything to do with the meteorology of the dream or the communication of repressed emotion. "Received" feelings could be entirely personal to the dreamworker, having no relation to the dream whatsoever. Again, we must suffer the discomfort of the unknown. I often envision myself sitting up to my neck in dark water, having to work on something invisible, underwater, by sensing only through my fingertips.

The dream-other whose mood the dreamworker absorbs does not necessarily have to be a *human* other. I showed this in the example of the man next to the refrigerator who transited into the freezer part of the refrigerator's interiority. It seems as if each particle of dreaming has an inner life. A transit is all it takes to experience it. We know this from creations closely related to dreaming, like myths and fairy tales, where brooks whisper, animals talk, and trees contemplate. Later Nganyinytja and Ilyatjari will show us around the inner life of a lizard, as we move along the dreaming tracks of the Ngintaka lizard.

In the dreamwork example I prepared for Ilyatjari, the dream-other is a balloon torn to shreds. I presented this case the week before in detailed lectures to Western audiences in Sydney and Melbourne, in order to have it freshly in my mind while talking to Ilyatjari. I want to get his response to a prime example of symbiotic communication. It concerns a dream of Monique's, a woman I worked with at Leiden University in the context of research done there on dream interpretation by an experimental psychologist. He presented the text of Monique's dream to several analysts from different schools of thought in Europe and the United States. (I don't know the final outcome of his study.) He invited me as the Jungian. I told him that, even though others were prepared to work exclusively from the text, without working with the dreamer, I would work only with the dreamer present.

Monique—the dreamer, whom I had never seen before —and I met in May of 1991, with the specific intention of working on her dream. We were meeting at Leiden University, my alma mater. Our work on the dream took fifty-five minutes and was conducted in Dutch.

I went into great detail, since I wanted to give Ilyatjari as clear an impression of my question about symbiotic communication as I possibly could, so he could not miss my point and would comment on it from his own cultural perspective.

Here I present the actual transcript of the audiotape and subsequent reflections I sent back to Leiden University for evaluation. My account to Ilyatjari was based on these materials. I told him the tale from faraway Holland on a warm August (winter) morning in the Center.

Monique and I talked for a few minutes before the work began, during which she told me she was five months pregnant—not that I hadn't noticed.

At my request, she told me her dream as much as possible from direct observation of the dream memory. I had first let her read through her written dream text, which had been sent around to all analysts in the study, and then asked her to return to the scene of the dream and report her direct observations. In this way she was able to give me a very involved report of the dream—from within, as it were. This offered me the opportunity to experience the dream along with her. (I did not read the dream text she had prepared for the other analysts in the study until a year later.)

I was bicycling on a little road and I was bicycling by myself, and at a certain moment I was being pushed off the road by a car. The car was driving very fast. So I was pushed off the road to the ground. And the car stopped just in front of me and that car was being chased by the police. Two policemen.

At a certain point I was in that car as well, and in that car there were two rascals and I was one of them, and I was behind the wheel and was driving, and to the left, next to my feet, I have a pistol on the floor, and in the back there are the policemen. In the car there is a lot of money. I had forgotten that, but when I read it again I remembered. The money was checks. Very handy. Ten checks. You just had to sign. And the money was hidden under the spare tire behind the backseat. It was real money, but you could only cash it two months from now. . . . No, you could only *spend* it in two months.

"You had the dream two months ago?" I ask, to make a first connection to the dream.

"Yes. So we're sitting in the car with the police in the back, and the police want to get to the pistol, and I was driving and I didn't want them to get it but I couldn't reach it. That's how we were driving. At a certain point we drove to my home. It is a very large mansion in a parklike setting, very beautifully landscaped. A very large house, and we enter and I was one of those rascals, and I was dressed in a very formal, tailor-made suit. My father used to call me "little rascal" as some kind of pet name. So I'm telling my butler, while he was going upstairs, what-all he had to prepare. He had to *make* all kinds of things. I was whispering to him, and the others didn't notice and we take the elevator up and at some point I pretend to have trouble walking, and then I told my rascal-partner: Does it occur to you that I have trouble walking? And my partner-scoundrel says, No, I can't see that. I did that to gain some time, 'cause I had whispered something to the butler for which he needed time. They went down again with the elevator and it took a long, long

time. And I was busy distracting these guys so they wouldn't notice that it was taking so long. And when we arrived, we got out of the elevator and I got into an air balloon with a basket, together with my partner-scoundrel, and we sat down in it comfortably and then the personnel had made a lot of wind and indeed the balloon rose up and it was a very liberating feeling. Then I looked up at the balloon above me and it was halfway torn, it was completely torn to shreds, and that made me laugh. That was the fun of it, and that's why it was working so well, because it had gone to shreds. Of course that was impossible, but it was a lot of fun, and it worked very well in that balloon and that basket and we really flew up in the air and you could see happy people everywhere. The police as well: they drove off so they were not chasing us. They were thinking that those were fun rascals after all. And then I saw a little girl on a farm for children, where you could play with the animals . . . and that was it.

I have a strong physical experience in my stomach when she mentions the balloon that is halfway torn to shreds. Her experience of the pleasantness of the balloon ride feels contradictory to my emotional experience. Whereas we both become absorbed in the atmosphere of the dream in the telling, she is feeling the upward, pleasant feelings while I am experiencing being torn to shreds inside my belly. My stomach had felt fine before she told me the dream. I suspect that I am feeling an element of the dream she is refusing to experience.

When first hearing a dream, I am usually discouraged by the incomprehensibility of the material the dreamer presents me with. I understand absolutely *nothing* of the dream. This feeling reflects the frustration of the rational mind, having to admit that it can't figure things out—and thereby leaving space for nonrational faculties. My complete lack of understanding used to make me feel horribly inferior, connecting as it did with a preset program of inferiority running in my family for generations. But after decades of dreamwork, that's all different now. Today it just makes me feel hopelessly inadequate and utterly unable to tackle the task of comprehending dreams.

All I actually know—or suspect—at the end of the telling of this dream is that there might be conflicting emotions around the balloon experience. I assume that the intense experience of shredding I feel in my stomach relates to an unconscious repression on the part of Monique. This gives direction to my strategy.

As a matter of method in my work on dreams I take it that a strategy can be devised for working through a dream. This strategy does not necessarily have us move through the dream from beginning to end, but tries instead to follow the subterranean emotional undercurrents present in the dream report. What is repressed most strongly may be the most important material, since it does not jibe with habitual consciousness. This material, if brought to consciousness, might dislocate the dreamer from her ruts, thus opening up fresh, new vistas.

Repression is not just a pressing down of emotion away from consciousness, it is at the same time the unconscious repulsion by means of which sensitive material fends off consciousness. This element of repression is called resistance. My usual strategy, therefore, is *to enter the dream at a point of low resistance—generally, an area in the dream where the dream-self feels comfortable—and move to a point of high resistance,* which is usually felt as discomfort. If we were to start out at the point of the highest resistance, the discomfort would instantly set up an impenetrable wall, to shield the dreamer from the pain caused by a confrontation with foreign elements of existence. The entire habitual psychological system is geared toward steering us clear of the unknown, even when we have the intention to face what we know not. Truly unknown wilderness frightens the habitual self. We are the convicts of our psychological habits. Therefore, the dreamer first needs a sense of safety before she can enter into more alien psychological territory. With each piece of dreamwork, then, whether I am working with someone for the first time or I have seen the dreamer over ten years of analysis, *I always try first to move to a safe place in the dreaming.* In a safe dream location the dreamer will have less resistance to her psychic surroundings. Entering into places of resistance too quickly might give rise to defenses of the habitual self against perceived danger. Therefore, it is sometimes unwise to work the dream in the chronological order of its narration. If the narrative opens at a point of high resistance, and ends in a safe place, it is better to work the dream backward. After entering at a point of low resistance, I slowly move toward the area of the dream where I sense the highest resistance. I cannot differentiate from the outset whether the indications I get belong to my subjectivity or to the dream. While listening to and working on a dream, I take shifts in my inner world as potential signposts. Sometimes they lead nowhere, sometimes I'm on track. I look for tracks in the wilderness of dreaming.

In this case I want to end up with the shredded balloon, since Monique's and my experiences of the balloon event are polar opposites—as if we were experiencing two contradicting forces inside the dreaming. This could point to a paradox. I've learned from C. G. Jung that the nodal

points of soul are the wringing knots of emotional contradiction. The tension of opposites, Jung teaches, is the
source of psychic energy. Whenever I suspect a paradox,
the least I can do is look.

In order to begin in a safe place, I start the work at the
moment when Monique is comfortably riding her bicycle
before all the pushing and shoving begins.

"So you're riding your bicycle . . ."

"Yes, I'm on my bike. Alone on a little road, a very
beautiful road, a bit romantic . . . I think I'm riding
home. . . . That car takes the corner. That's where I'm
pushed off the road."

"Just before you get to that bend," I ask, "how do you
feel?" In this way I establish a relationship between the
dreamer and myself in a safe place.

"I'm very contented. I'm riding at ease," she replies. The
sense of ease in the dreamworld is at the same time a sense
of ease with my presence. The atmosphere between us
feels relaxed. A few minutes later, then, the police can be
introduced.

The collective image of police exists in context for everyone. Before I enter the image in depth I have to know
Monique's conscious associations regarding policemen.
Once the dreamwork has achieved a certain depth it will
be disturbing to ask context questions, since these may
lead the dreamer back to surface consciousness.

"It has to do with my parents, maybe," she responds to
my question about police. "They are rather judgmental.
They're judging my spouse, Karel. Karel looks like the
other scoundrel. . . . They always *inspect* people. Nothing
is ever good enough. They say Karel is lazy. Very ex-
treme. Partially true, though . . ."

Now we have two aspects of "police" on this surface

level: the parents who are pushy and judgmental, and Monique's own judgmental side, agreeing with her parents' assessment of Karel.

To feel the pushy side more, I ask, "The police push you off the road?"

"Yes! . . . I fall."

An implicit subliminal connection has been made between police, parents, pushy, and falling down. "I am forced to drive by the police, who're in the back of the car," Monique recalls.

As the dreamworker I feel a sense of oppression settling in when we enter into the dream car. This policed air is thick with compulsion. I wait.

"I wonder how I can get rid of the police," she contemplates out loud.

"How does it feel when you do?" I ask, moving the action forward.

"It is just wonderful, a real liberation."

I feel the oppression lift as my breath comes more easily.

"Relief?" I ask.

"Yes!"

With the use of the Dutch word *opluchting*, meaning "relief" but consisting of the images of "upward" (*op*) and "air" (*lucht*), I have introduced a poetic metaphor calling up the atmosphere of the air balloon. At first ballooning upward appears in the dreamwork only as a brief impression; later it will become more fully fleshed out.

But I want us to feel again the oppression of the police(d) car, and the relief at the thought of getting rid of them. We have to experience both atmospheres, tense and relieved, until we can feel them *viscerally*, as distinct physical responses. This can be achieved by an intensification of pressure. We can intensify the pressure by concentrating our focus on the image. Concentration of focus gathers emotional attention in a single point. Such focused emotions are accompanied by corresponding physical sensations.

"So there is great tension when the police are after you?"

"Yes, a great restriction in my freedom."

"How does that feel in your body?"

She sits bent over, feeling the restriction.

"Just like I'm sitting now . . . like a straitjacket."

I let the straitjacket feeling—which I had felt before, as a first impression when with her inside the police(d) car— resonate for a few moments through our bodies. After some time spent in concentration, the oppression is anchored as a physical sensation in the body. It feels, physically, like being in a straitjacket. I now import corresponding emotions from her daytime memories into the dreaming atmosphere in order to amplify the emotional signal.

"Do you know this straitjacket feeling?" I ask.

"Yes, that's the way I feel when I'm not accepted. I feel this very strongly from my parents. They judge me. I'm an only child. They have this ideal—well-adjusted, well-behaved, what will the neighbors think, pretty, nice girl to talk to . . ."

I feel a very sharp pain cut through my belly. It feels like a sympathetic response of my own system to the increasing pressure she is experiencing while thinking of her painfully restricted upbringing. The import has strengthened the straitjacket signal.

"How do you feel in your belly?" I ask her point-blank, at the risk of being intrusive or of suggesting sensations to her that may not be present. I ask my question directly, but in a tone that is open-ended. The pressure in the dreamwork is increasing.

"Oppressive," she replies. "Frightening. Pain is coming up."

We have reached the somatic essence of the straitjacket feeling, in the same way we essentialized coldness in the refrigerator dreamwork. You could cut the tension in the room with a knife. I now effect decompression once again by using the word *opluchting*, "relief"—once again calling back the moment, a short while back, when the use of this same word had brought relief. I say, "You are in a car with the police. You feel caught in a straitjacket and you think, how do I get relief [*opluchting*]?" This affords us a breather. In dreamwork we constantly modulate pressure in order to keep a balance between the imperative of the dreamwork to press deeper into the sensitive areas that repel consciousness and the need of the dreamer to feel safe. We come up to the surface, from the depth of the belly.

"Yes." Her voice comes out in a deep breath.

"You try to get to the place of relief."

Decompression has occurred, yet we shouldn't lose all pressure and relax entirely; otherwise, we will lose the closeness to the straitjacket sensations in the belly. "Can you feel the police behind you?" I ask. With this inquiry I move us to a focus behind her back. Action behind our backs makes us feel vulnerable, unaware of what's really going on. It keeps us off balance.

"They're very attentive. They want to keep the situation under control. They feel that it is difficult."

We're now both sitting with our eyes closed, concentrating on the policemen in the back of the car. At this

point I attempt to shift perspective—to transit from the
dream-self to the dream police.

"Do they feel frustrated?" I inquire.

"Yes, they're frustrated as well, because they no longer
have control over the situation."

"Can you try to sense what they are feeling right now?"

"They're very insecure. Because these rascals have some
kind of gun. Poof!" She makes a noise of a gunshot.

"How does that fear feel?"

"Very threatening."

"What does it feel like to them?"

"It's a sign of their own insecurities."

"They need to be secure. [In Dutch, the word *secure* also
means "certain."] How is it to live with all these insecurities, uncertainties?"

"Very insecure." She giggles, insecure. "It feels like a
straitjacket as well."

"So they are in a straitjacket just like you?"

"Yes, but much worse." Monique has felt her way into
one of the policemen through an active use of empathy.
She has entered the atmosphere of the policeman's world.
Now she slowly "becomes" the policeman, moving from
empathy to identification. In this way, the interior life of
the police is experienced directly.

"Let's continue with that," I suggest. "*How* are they in a
straitjacket? You are a policeman and they are sitting in
the back and you're riding with the rascals and you're very
insecure. They have a pistol." The movement from empathy to identification is aided by my ambiguous use of the
word *they*. The first and second *they's* still refer to the policemen, from an outside perspective; the third *they* refers
to the rascals from the policeman's point of view. This

ambiguous use of personal pronouns can be very effective in the transition from empathy to identification.

"Yes," she concurs. "Then I'm very insecure and you look for security by exercising power, because of your own insecurity."

Her use of the pronoun *you*—a generalizing term—shows that Monique's identification with the policeman is not yet complete. To achieve complete identification, I return us to the somatic experience.

I ask, "Where in your body can you feel this insecurity [this uncertainty] that makes you want to exercise power?"

Monique points to the lower part of her belly, then to a place a little higher, where the discomfort had previously been located. "Here, but not there," she replies. The straitjacket-powerdrive-parental emotion is now firmly anchored as an ache deep in the belly. The feeling has become clearly recognizable as a physical sensation each of us feels in our belly—and it is possible for the moment for us to take it as a somatic benchmark sensation with which to explore her *daily* life. Exporting as well as importing are vital moves in dreamwork. We export the essentialized straitjacket feeling to her day life to engender fresh insights. These insights, in turn, bring up corresponding emotions that may be imported back to the dreamworld.

"Do you know moments in your life," I inquire, "when you suddenly become police, where you become very insecure and begin to exercise power?"

"I have been extremely insecure, but I *can't* exercise power. Instead I surrender entirely. I lose myself."

"How does it feel to lose yourself?" Apparently there is a connection between the straitjacket sensation and the loss of identity and power.

"Very creepy," she responds. (The Dutch word used is

eng, which in addition to "creepy" also means "tight, nar-row," like a straitjacket). "I was very depressed and ran away from home." What she says feels similar to that of her depressed husband, Karel. "I was with my first boy-friend, but I didn't know whether he was after me or my mother. I was so insecure. I was lying on my bed, totally apathetic. I couldn't do a thing. At a certain point I came back to myself by observing very carefully whether I was feeling cold or warm. Then I came back to my own feel-ing. Then the relationship broke up. I found my own iden-tity. This is all related to my marriage with Karel. Whether to go on or not."

Monique has already previously connected her sense of identity to a somatic experience—"feeling cold or warm" —which encourages me to continue with my body-fo-cused approach. At the same time, her current marital di-lemma is now viewed in the broader context of the paren-tal straitjacket/loss-of-identity/powerlessness complex.

"This apathy you're talking about," I pursue, "is it similar to your husband's, recently?"

"Yes, that's true," she confirms. "He has a total loss of confidence. He has lost his identity. He has a hard time with my pregnancy and being responsible for a family."

At this moment Monique realizes that she can't stand Karel's apathy because of her own tendency toward it. Here we pause.

Now we have experienced the judgmental, parental po-lice force biographically, somatically, and in the current marital tension. It feels like we have completed a piece of dreamwork on the image of police. It is time to return to the dream—but, as in a musical concert, there is a pause between two movements.

I decide to reenter the dream at another place related to

the sense of identity: the checks that required a signature. This element of the dream had been forgotten up until the moment she presented the dream to me. ("I had forgotten that, but when I read it again I remembered.") Such forgetting *may* point to repression, when material is pushed away from consciousness. It's worth a closer look.

"The money in the car is money for which you have to put a signature."

Monique laughs. "Yes, they were checks. Stolen money."

"What is your association to signature?"

"My father forged my signature."

"Oh?"

Monique laughs again. I am completely taken aback by this bit of biography, which has turned up so unexpectedly while we're exploring Monique's sense of identity by way of her own signature.

"I was in Germany," she explains, "and wanted to buy a house. I had bought the house already. My father was going to cosign. Later, it turned out that this wouldn't even have been necessary. At the last moment, my father wrote a letter to the broker stating that I didn't have the money. He signed it with my signature. When I came back to Holland two weeks later, I heard that the deal had fallen through."

I feel an intense upsurge of outrage. I feel totally violated.

"What did you feel?"

"I felt a little bit betrayed. You don't do that to someone you love."

This understatement comes across to me as a denial of the strong emotions her father's violation must have caused.

"Did it feel criminal to you?" I ask, to connect the event with the police/rascal image.

"Yes. Of course, I could have gone to court, but I didn't want to. But I felt totally tricked. It was very difficult."

I feel the anger changing to sadness. Tears come to my eyes.

"There is sadness," I remark.

"Insecurity." She begins to cry. "It isn't fair. First my mother who takes my boyfriend away, then my father. It hurts."

I let her feel the hurt. We are silent. The pain feels very sharp.

I feel a desire for momentary relief. "Shall we go to the air balloon?" I ask. We both laugh. The tension is broken. Monique's face, which has been contorted with pain, clears up instantly. Maybe we can feel the shredding of the balloon now that she has experienced her father's betrayal.

"It is shot to shreds," I observe. "Life is shot to shreds time and again. You're sitting in a balloon shot to shreds." In my eagerness to push her toward the experience of shredding, I have unconsciously added a shot, never fired in the dream—a potential shot from the gun lying on the police car's floor at the foot of the driving rascal.

"I feel very relieved. It goes up higher and higher. It feels very good." Instead of feeling discomfort she goes up and out.

"It feels like flight," I offer. "A flight from the police?"

The pun makes her laugh. There is more relief, more breaking of tension. I realize that my timing in attempting to get to the shredding is off. Pushy eagerness often leads to the opposite of what it tries to accomplish. Also, pushy isn't quite what she needs after a life of overbearing parental policing. We have to back up, and rebuild the tension to a higher level of pressure, to get to the point where the shredded balloon can experience itself, by means of a transit from Monique to the torn balloon.

"I want to return to the point where you're talking to the butler," I recommence. "Where is that taking place?" I feel like we're starting from scratch. We have to submerge all over again.

"When we enter the house."

Because of my poor timing, pushing for the torn feelings too early, we're back in surface consciousness, having to *enter* the image all over again. The spontaneous emergence of a dream moment of entrance is fortunate.

At this point, we have a discussion about the richness of the house—not a feature of her biography—and her parents' expectations that she become successful—hence their disapproval of Karel—followed by an exploration of ways in which the image of success and wealth helps her avoid a sense of insecurity.

"Could you say something about three-piece suits?" I ask.

"When I was in Germany I was very well dressed. I think it served to mask my insecurity. When I'm well dressed I feel more adjusted." She giggles, a little embarrassed.

After about five more minutes of this I refocus on the dream to take the final approach to the shredded balloon. We are forty-five minutes into the dreamwork. I want to finish in less than sixty minutes, to remain realistic in this session—conducted for the purpose of academic research—in terms of the maximum time a therapist usually gets to spend.

"So the butler sees to it that you can get away?"

"Yes, together with the rest of the personnel."

"Is this the first time that you employ his services to escape?"

"No. He's helped me escape more than once," she remembers for sure, as though this dream butler had been a familiar figure in her life. "At this moment I feel glad to get out of that suffocating situation." I surmise I'm faced with a habitual escape mechanism that serves to get rid of a sense of suffocation, to get air.

"What is the air balloon like?"

"It is quite a big basket. It is fun. Like a vacation."

"Tell me about vacations."

Monique laughs. "I leave everything behind."

She sounds as if she hasn't a care in the world, and laughs again. Maybe through direct contrast I can get her to feel the suffocation she leaves behind in the airy balloon.

"And the balloon is shredded to bits?" I venture.

"Yes, half of it. That's the strange thing about it. It is billowing in the wind."

"And the wind is being made by the butler and the personnel? How?"

"Yes. I'm not sure how. With huge machines, I think. It was well organized and ready in time. It took a lot of people to deploy them." We both laugh. Laughter at this stage seems to indicate that we are reaching difficult material we *want* to laugh off.

"So it takes a lot of energy to fly away?"

It seems to take a lot of energy to escape. The whole escape mechanism is organized to move Monique up and out.

"Yes. But I'm just standing in the elevator going down." She laughs, making it clear that it doesn't cost *her* any energy. She is still. The personnel are doing all the work, she isn't doing a thing, she is innocent. There is an emphatic identification with the dream-self, an unconscious effort by Monique to put a distance between herself and the complex that laboriously, mechanically, enables escape. She's not responsible for this escape mechanism, which would indicate that it functions autonomously, automatically, habitually.

"In the elevator going down," I repeat to emphasize a movement away from the high flight of the balloon.

"Yes, for a long time we keep on going down."

"How does that feel?"

"A tense situation."

"Can you concentrate on the elevator going down?"

"I feel pressure."

"What's that like?"

"Suffocating. Yes, great pressure. I think I'm getting sick. Physically sick. Powerless."

"Have you ever had cyclical phases when you become very depressed and then high?" I want to emphasize the contrast between up and down, mania and depression.

"I used to. Very strongly. I would get sick."

I realize I am having trouble breathing. It feels as though the straitjacket were now inside my lungs. "How do your lungs feel?" I ask, to verify whether it is just me, or if this is a symbiotic response.

"Suffocating!" She coughs uncontrollably.

"Now I understand why they have to make so much air," I interpret, "because the pressure is so unbearable. That way you get some air again, but at the same time you shoot up." I employ reason to relieve the tension one notch, to move her out of her coughing fit. What I had previously employed implicitly through the use of the word *opluchting* (upward, air, relief), I fully flesh out at this point.

"At a certain point we are no longer moving up. First we go up, then to the side. That's the fun." Tension is released.

"How high are you?"

"Like that tree," she says, pointing outside.

"One more thing," I say, gathering all the focus I can muster into my voice, "and then we'll have to stop." By saying this, I let her know that she will only have to deal with my question for a brief moment—for now.

"Can you feel what it is like to be torn to shreds?"

"That seems terrible to me."

"What does it feel like?" I repeat, feeling the density of the moment. We are in a realm of reality where experience is extremely concentrated.

"Like *nothing*." She sits with her hands in her lap, with a ravaged expression, feeling annihilated.

"Do you ever feel like nothing?" I pursue.

"Yes. Then I become ill. Not angry or anything like that." She laughs nervously, indicating that she wants to leave this torn-up wasteland. While she is experiencing the depth of her distress, my belly feels at peace, for the first time since she told me the dream.

"Let's stop here," I suggest.

"Yes. I find it very good how you can take a person along in such a dream, in the experience." She sounds grateful. Probably both for the work as well as for stopping it.

When, a year later, I was presented with the translated English text of the dream the other analysts had been given for interpretation, it spoke only of half a balloon, with no mention about it having been torn to shreds. She remembered this aspect only while recalling her dream from inside, in her presentation to me. It had been part of the dreaming, she had just forgotten about it until then. The memory of the balloon being torn had been repressed.

This dreamwork had a peculiar tail end. As if the dream were precognitive, a few months later, in the eighth month of her pregnancy, well before the due date, Monique got up in the morning with the feeling that something was wrong. Her husband tried to calm her down; he didn't want her to go to the healer she had been seeing for a while in addition to her doctors. But she trusted herself enough to insist with her husband, to push herself through—and saw the healer. Monique wrote to me after reading the material and comments I had sent back to the Leiden University research psychologist:

> This healer tells me that my intuition is correct and that it is important to induce labor as soon as possible! The gynecologist and her assistants take echograms etc., but don't find any reason to induce labor early, but it is finally decided to follow my intuition and break the water. The umbilical cord tears at the first contraction. After reading your piece I felt a strong connection between the torn balloon and the torn umbilical cord.

The doctors said that if she had not followed her sense of her own body, and her instinct, the umbilical cord might have torn in the womb, which could have meant death for both mother and child. It had already been very fragile before the birth.

● ● ●

"Has he ever experienced such feelings in himself that belong to his patients?" I ask, looking at Ilyatjari, full of expectation.

Consternation among the Pitjantjatjara. Ilyatjari the ngankari looks flustered. There is an intense discussion between him and Diana, our interpreter. *She* blushes and looks sheepish.

"This is my fault," she says. "I should have told you. But he doesn't deal with women's issues like pregnancy. That is something for the *woman* ngankari to deal with. It is strange to him that *you* deal with it."

We are all embarrassed.

CHAPTER 5

Dreaming Tracks

AS I CAST ABOUT FOR ANOTHER EXAMPLE OF SYMBIOTIC COMMUNI-
cation, all I draw is a blank. I have been so taken aback by
Ilyatjari's response that I don't know what to say. Finally I
come up with some lame example of a case where I felt in
my knee an aggressive urge to kick—and subsequently discovered a great deal of aggression hidden within the
dream.

Ilyatjari, his wife Nganyinytja, and their sister-in-law
talk among themselves. No, they conclude, they don't recognize this experience in the knee. They repeat their own
symbiotic grammar: twitch in the nose for a stranger, hip
for a spouse, upper arm for aunt or sister, etc. They don't
have such feelings in their knees. It must be idiosyncratic
to me. I don't know whether they have not understood me
or if they actually don't recognize my brand of so-called
symbiotic communication.

There is a long silence.

I regroup my thoughts. I want to know more about Ilyatjari's life as an eagle. I want to find out if this experience
is some kind of lucid dreaming, like my Leiden Academy

dream. I want to check whether he knows that he is dreaming while he flies as an eagle at night. But how to ask?

Lucidity, dreaming while being aware of the dream state, is a relatively rare occurrence in its spontaneous form. In my experience, it happens to a minority of people and then only infrequently. Even with those dreamers who train their abilities to become lucid, I would guess that of the twenty years of dreaming during a lifetime, lucid dream time wouldn't cover a month. Since my Leiden Academy dream I have been interested in lucidity for the opportunity it offers to experience the absolute reality of the dreaming environment.

"Can you ask him if he knows that his body is in his bed while he is flying like an eagle?"

"No one can steal from the ngankari while he is away. That is very dangerous for the thief."

It sounds like a non sequitur. Maybe his trance is so deep that a taboo has to surround him to protect him: while he is an eagle he is taboo. I have spoken with native Hawaiians about their *kapu* system, which makes one who possesses a great deal of power (*mana*) taboo (*kapu*) for mere mortals. He or she can't be touched, at the risk of instant death to the one who does so.

I don't consider the possibility that the ngankari might actually be *away*, off flying to the Milky Way. I cannot conceive of a physical eagle flight. I believe that his flight through the stars takes place in a parallel reality: that of a City of Light, of a *mundus imaginalis*, a world consisting of true substance, the nature of which is fundamentally unknown.

My tangential reflections on *mana* and *kapu* don't bring me any closer to an answer. How do I get a handle on the

nature of Ilyatjari's consciousness as he flies through the
cosmos? Does he stay entirely inside the eagle world, or
does he know that he exists in two worlds simultaneously
—a world of eagle and a world of human body? I am
fumbling around for another approach when Ilyatjari
breaks into my thoughts.

"Give me another example," he proposes, curious about
our joint intellectual inquiry.

I decide to tell them last night's dream.

**My dream last night took place in my home in Holland. I am
in the living room with my mother. There are wide doors. [I
don't know how to describe sliding French doors to the
ngankari.] My uncle comes in from the other room and
stands in the door opening. He is dressed in a 1920s cos-
tume, with knickerbockers, the way he would go to Mardi
Gras. [I decide to just tell what I remember and give up on
the hope that Ilyatjari will understand all of it. I pity the
interpreter.] There is an argument between him and my
mother. It is about something he thinks is fun but which
offends my mother. I take my uncle's side and get annoyed
with my mother. I decide to leave, and am on the verge of
stomping out when I notice my father at the entrance to the
room. I know that he had been very ill and had almost died,
but hadn't, and that I haven't seen him for months. I decide
to stay, and take my father by the hand, over to the couch. I
sit next to him and embrace him, telling him how much I
love him.**

As I tell this I become emotional again, as I was in the
dream. Nganyinytja looks at me lovingly. I swallow the
lump in my throat. My father had been absent from my

dreams for many months. I realize how much I've missed him.

I pull myself together. "Now, while I was dreaming this, I was here, in Australia. But I didn't *know* that I was in Australia. I was sure I was in Holland. Can you ask him whether he knows that his body is asleep on Earth while he flies to the Milky Way?"

It takes Diana some time to translate my final question. Again there seems to be some confusion.

"He can't travel that far," Diana relays.

"What do you mean?" I exclaim.

"Dreams for him are about travel. The soul travels. And he can't travel all the way to Holland. It is too far for him."

Here is a man who travels to the center of the galaxy, but Holland is too distant for him! I feel far away from home indeed.

"Your father is dead?" Nganyinytja asks. I nod. Ilyatjari says something. Nganyinytja talks at the same time. Diana is flustered.

"He wants to know about your question. He wants to understand your question about when he flies. She wants to know if you miss your father. She says that the dream is about the fact that you didn't do something for your father's funeral. Maybe you weren't there, and he comes to remind you that you still have to do some rites or other."

My father died while I was on the plane to Holland from Moscow, after I had been told of his heart attack. I remember my mother opening the door, saying, "Too late, you're too late!"

I tell Nganyinytja of this recollection. She is moved. We talk more about my father. Perhaps because in the previous night's dream I'd sided against my mother, I now

follow Nganyinytja's interest and ask her about
Pitjantjatjara funeral rites, disregarding Ilyatjari and our inquiry into the nature of dreaming consciousness. He
stomps off, annoyed. You could cut the tension between
them with a knife.

There can be only one conclusion:

Marriage is the same wherever you go!

We never returned to the question regarding the nature of
Ilyatjari's eagle consciousness. He answered my question
half a year later, though, when I wrote to Nganyinytja and
him to ask for their permission to use the material they
had presented to me—since I believe that whatever indig-
enous people present to Westerners should be considered
as inherently copyrighted material. While granting me
permission, Ilyatjari pointed to one mistake I had made: I
had described his flight as an Eagle Dreaming. After reading him the text I'd sent, Diana James, our gifted intermediary, wrote back:

"Referring to the ngankari flight as an eagle carrying
people for healing cannot be referred to as 'Eagle Dreaming.' Ngankaris do not consider they are dreaming when
they fly, nor is this method referred to as a *Tjukurpa*—a
Dreaming about the eagle."

The second part of his correction is immediately obvious: a Dreaming in the sense of *Tjukurpa* refers to the creative activity of a primordial being leaving lore and landscape in its wake. Primordial land, it is believed, was
wholly without features. Land*scape* came into being
through the dreaming adventures of the likes of Ngintaka,
the lizard whose dreamtime footsteps we are to follow
later on. Comparable to the creative lives of the dreaming
geniuses manifesting the dreamworlds of the night,

Dreaming in the sense of *Tjukurpa* portrays the lives of the creative geniuses of the space-time we live in while awake.

His first correction is more subtle—and in fact answers my question. No, his eagle flight is not a lucid dream. It is a movement through time and space different from ordinary dreaming. This already becomes clear from the fact that the patient participates in the same flight, so the ngankari and the patient have a common experience. Two people sharing a single dreaming is not part of an ordinary dream experience. I, for one, have never encountered totally identical shared dreaming among the many people who've told me their dreams. Similarities, yes; identical, no.

Now I also understand his strange answer about stealing from the ngankari's camp while he is on his flight, when I asked him if he knows that he is dreaming in his camp while flying as an eagle. As far as he is concerned, he is truly absent from his camp while flying as an eagle. There is a seamless continuum between material and nonmaterial time and space. *Time and space are essential, matter incidental.* Ilyatjari appears not to differentiate between a material and a nonmaterial presence of space-time.

We retreat to our camps before Nganyinytja will guide us on the dreaming trail (*Tjukurpa*) to follow the lizard (Ngintaka), whose primordial existence created this landscape. Diana had prearranged this outing with our bush teachers, in order to help us grasp the nature of dreaming, and the dreaming of nature. As I lie down, the dream of the White House and the nonpterodactyls comes back to me. My Western mind wants to resist the primordial birds. Something is driving me crazy.

I find some comfort in the fact that I'm part of a tradition of analysts afraid to be driven crazy by primeval wilderness. The following is an excerpt from C. G. Jung's memoirs, *Memories, Dreams, Reflections*, taken from the chapter "Kenya and Uganda," a report of Jung's confrontation with the primordial in the heart of Africa. It is 1925. Jung is fifty years old.

When the first ray of sunlight announced the onset of day, I awoke. The train, swathed in a red cloud of dust, was just making a turn around a steep red cliff. On a jagged rock above us a slim, brownish-black figure stood motionless, leaning on a long spear, looking down at the train. Beside him towered a gigantic candelabrum cactus.

I was enchanted by this sight—it was a picture of something utterly alien and outside my experience, but on the other hand a most intense *sentiment du déjà vu.* I had the feeling that I had already experienced this moment and had always known this world which was separated from me only by distance in time. It was as if I were this moment returning to the land of my youth, and as if I knew that dark-skinned man who had been waiting for me for five thousand years.

The feeling-tone of this curious experience accompanied me throughout my whole journey through savage Africa. I can recall only one other such recognition of the immemorially known. That was when I first observed a parapsychological phenomenon, together with my former chief, Professor Eugen Bleuler. Beforehand I had imagined that I would be dumbfounded if I were to see so fantastic a thing. But when it happened, I was not surprised at all; I felt it was perfectly natural, something I could take for granted because I had long since been acquainted with it. [I'm reminded of Nganyinytja's matter-of-fact description of Pitjantjatjara parapsychology.]

I could not guess what string within myself was plucked at the sight of that solitary dark hunter. I knew only that his world had been mine for countless millennia.

Somewhat bemused, I arrived around noon in Nairobi, situated at an altitude of six thousand feet. . . .

From Nairobi we used a small Ford to visit the Athi Plains, a great game preserve. From a low hill in this broad savanna a magnificent prospect opened out to us. To the very brink of the horizon we saw gigantic herds of animals: gazelle, antelope, gnu, zebra, warthog, and so on. Grazing, heads nodding, the herds moved forward like slow rivers. There was scarcely any sound save the melancholy cry of a bird of prey. This was the stillness of the eternal beginning, the world as it had always been, in the state of non-being; for until then no one had been present to know that it was this world. I walked away from my companions until I had put them out of sight, and savored the feeling of being entirely alone. There I was now, the first human being to recognize that this was the world, but who did not know that in this moment he had first really created it.

There the cosmic meaning of consciousness became overwhelmingly clear to me. "What nature leaves imperfect, the art perfects," say the alchemists. Man, I, in an invisible act of creation put the stamp of perfection on the world by giving it objective existence. . . . Human consciousness created objective existence and meaning, and man found his indispensable place in the great process of being. . . . [Is this the white-housed Western mind of objectivity speaking, observing a background of primordial, archaic existence?]

Our camp life proved to be one of the loveliest interludes in my life. I enjoyed the "divine peace" of a still primeval country. Never had I seen so clearly "man and the other animals" (Herodotus). Thousands of miles lay between me and Europe, mother of all demons. The demons could not reach me here—there were no telegrams, no telephone calls, no letters, no visitors. My liberated psychic forces poured blissfully back to the primeval expanses. . . .

In general the people asseverated that the Creator had made everything good and beautiful. He was beyond good and evil. He was *m'zuri,* that is, beautiful, and everything he did was *m'zuri.*

When I asked: "But what about the wicked animals who kill your cattle?" they said, "The lion is good and beautiful." "And your horrible diseases?" They said, "You lie in the sun and it is good."

I was impressed by this optimism. But at six o'clock in the evening this optimism was suddenly over, as I soon discovered. From sunset on, it was a different world—the dark world of *ayik,* of evil, danger, fear. The optimistic philosophy gave way to fear of ghosts and magical practices intended to secure protection from evil. Without any inner contradiction the optimism returned at dawn. . . .

During the entire trip my dreams stubbornly followed the tactic of ignoring Africa. They drew exclusively upon scenes from home, and thus seemed to say that they considered—if it is permissible to personify the unconscious processes to this extent—the African journey not as something real, but rather as a symptomatic or symbolic act. Even the most impressive events of the trip were rigorously excluded from my dreams. Only once during the entire expedition did I dream of a Negro. His face appeared curiously familiar to me, but I had to reflect a long time before I could determine where I had met him before. Finally it came to me: he had been my barber in Chattanooga, Tennessee! An American Negro. *In the dream he was holding a tremendous, red-hot curling iron to my head, intending to make my hair kinky—that is, to give me*

Negro hair. I could already feel the painful heat, and awoke with a sense of terror. [italics mine]

I took this dream as a warning from the unconscious; it was saying that the primitive was a danger to me. At that time I was obviously all too close to "going black." I was suffering an attack of sandfly fever which probably reduced my psychic resistance. In order to represent a Negro threatening me, my unconscious had invoked a twelve-year-old memory of my Negro barber in America, just in order to avoid any reminder of the present.

This curious behavior of my dreams corresponds, incidentally, to a phenomenon which was noted during the First World War. Soldiers in the field dreamt far less of the war than of their homes. Military psychiatrists considered it a basic principle that a man should be pulled out of the front lines when he started dreaming too much of war scenes, for that meant he no longer possessed any psychic defenses against the impressions from outside.

Parallel to my involvement with this demanding African environment, an interior line was being successfully secured within my dreams. The dreams dealt with my personal problems. The only thing I could conclude from this was that my European personality must under all circumstances be preserved intact. . . .

The trip revealed itself as less an investigation of primitive psychology . . . than a probing into the rather embarrassing question: What is going to happen to Jung the psychologist in the wilds of Africa?

I want to look at Jung's dream from the point of view of the "barber in Chattanooga, Tennessee." He sees a white man with short-cropped, straight white hair, an older man. Jung's black dreamworld barber wants Jung to have hair

like him, have a head like him—possibly to think like him,
envision the world like him. The barber knows that the
unknown world is full of demons, frightening forces
greater than man, "the dark world of *ayik,* of evil, danger,
fear"—forces that have access to us at will, who can manifest themselves if it is their pleasure, who may torture us if
they so wish. They live all around us—not, as Western
man would believe it, inside our skulls. The white man
would have gone out of his head.

In dreamwork, we would have listened to Jung's reasons
for his defense against the black man. By association, he
felt himself in a state of warfare inside this primordial
world, in a "psychic defense . . . against the impressions
from outside," a replay of the Great World War of seven
years before. We would feel the danger and the fear.

Then we might move our attention to the dream barber,
a stand-in for the African who is related to "a picture of
something utterly alien and outside my experience, but on
the other hand [provoking] a most intense *sentiment du déjà
vu.*" We'd observe his movements, how he walks around in
his Tennessee barbershop. What the atmosphere is in the
barbershop. How he feels in this atmosphere, in his body.

Then we would enter the desire to give the white man
kinks in his hair. How the gigantic, glowing curling iron
feels in the hand. Does he want to endanger the white
man? What does he want? Maybe he wants to convey
something. Some tremendous, red-hot issue. The white
man is terrified—the Chattanooga dreamworld disinte-
grates and the white man wakes up, sick, in Africa, the
land of the birth of humanity, waiting for him to return for
well over five thousand years.

Meeting with primordial consciousness is frightening. It
threatens to burn the straight white mind.

There is still half an hour before we leave on the dreaming trail. I close my eyes and doze off.

In the other world, I am taken to a lower place on a dreaming track. The dorsal fin of a landshark is following my wife. It is the familiar black triangle of *Jaws,* now cutting its way through the sands of the camel-colored desert. Very scary. I might have screamed.

A shift of worlds: in another world, one of my students is very upset about the changes occurring in the way I work. She is annoyed that I taught one way and now change my mind. Everyone can do with their work as they please, I say. . . .

My student mentality is distraught. The mind is changing.

Children are playing. The blond little white boy is wrapped in a yellow blanket, like a ghost in a medieval play. He is surrounded by ten Pitjantjatjara kids. The children push and shove and laugh in delight. Thin legs and running noses follow us as we walk away from the camp for a few minutes, just before we leave to track the lizard whose dreaming brought into existence this sunlit land of scraggy mountains afloat in a placid ocean of red rocks and dry trees.

Before the dreaming ancestors—like the lizard Ngintaka —came, the land was dull and formless. Australian land-scape came to be because the ancestors of yore were dreaming it. They moved through the dreamworld, called the Dreaming, or *Tjukurpa,* experiencing adventures written down in the landscape as a text for those literate in dreaming tracks to read. The landscape is like a dream log that the beings of the dreamtime kept, to serve as a remembrance solidified in stone, making their exploits eternally present.

By following the path of Ngintaka, the lizard (*Perentie varanus gigantus*), we enter a world he left behind to be remembered by. And it is the task of Aboriginal people to remember; otherwise the Dreaming dies out of the landscape, something that has already happened with the Western mind. "For Western consciousness," says Dr. David Tacey, "the landscape is apparently barren, empty, unalive. The Western intellectual view is not sure whether there is a real Aboriginal landscape at all, or whether our experience of that landscape is entirely constructed. All we can know according to the intellectual position are our own internal images, which we anthropomorphically project upon the face of the earth so that the earth bears or carries our own face." One of the central Western notions maintains that everything outside of the human is soulless.

Not so to Nganyinytja. She is responsible for the land. Now in her sixties, until her twelfth year she and her family roamed the outback, never seeing a European, living a life reaching back eons. Her family had to tend this land, sing the landscape its song so it could reflect on its existence.

The quiet mountains never change. Who enters the landscape enters its imagination, its atmosphere, its story. We will follow the *Perentie* lizard, Ngintaka, finding ourselves inside the dreaming imagination of Ngintaka. We are part of his dreaming. He is the dreaming "I" who lives the story we will participate in for forty kilometers across the ancestral land Nganyinytja now stewards.

It is an odd experience to be inside someone else's dreaming, especially a lizard's. My Western ego protests. It has always been the center of its own dreaming, its perspective the one from which dreaming was experienced. Who wants to be an extra in the imaginings of a lizard? Haven't *I* been contracted for the lead?

Like the bow of a ship, a large red boulder sails through waves of rocks that seem to break away like rusted ice. Where the bow meets the surrounding rocks, two little caves are formed. Nganyinytja and her sister-in-law break into song, drumming music sticks together in the rhythm of a heartbeat. The voices are nasal, and like the landscape: flat, with occasional rises in craggy counterpoint.

Diana translates. "Ngintaka is in the cave there, having a bit of a nap, when he hears the others who've been following him coming. He hears them talking about him." Apparently we have entered a story in the middle, as would befit dreaming, which is discontinuous in nature. Dreaming is a collection of moments.

This is a paranoid moment in the landscape, a chase. "They're talking about me!" Here Ngintaka feels threatened.

It is up to our guides to sing the song and do the dance to bring to life the interior experience of this spot. They are doing dreamwork, as it were, with Ngintaka. They relive the chase and become infused by the meaning of this particular place. Ngintaka lives! We are in his dreaming.

Unlike the cabdriver in my lucid Leiden Academy dream, I seem to accept that I live in another's dreaming. Wilderness begins to enter me.

The vegetation changes. Trees around us become higher as the Toyota bumps along an invisible course through the wild. I'd love to drive this terrain. On our left we see a wild camel grazing in an almost dry salt lake. A sandflat with muddy rivulets where birds bathe their reddish-purple chests is all that is left of Ngintaka's playground: here behind the mountains, he had shaken off his pursuers, hid his stolen bounty—apparently he had stolen a flat grinding stone, thus the hot pursuit: "Follow that Ngintaka!"— and relaxed in this safe place, rolling wantonly on his belly, enjoying the mud and creating the salt lake with his tail. I could envision the giant *Perentie* rolling on his belly like a dog in the snow or a pig in the mud. The sensuous pleasure of the place is palpable.

On the far side of the "lake," the hay-colored grass is burnt black. Ilyatjari did this a month ago. He does it before the rains, so the grass can grow green again and the kangaroo may feed. This eco-stewardship is no more or less important than the song that is now reminding us of Ngintaka's delight.

I can almost feel it in my skin. The clicks, high and clear, of the women's music sticks sing the song of a beating heart. Inside Ngintaka's dreaming, the body purrs with well-being. The calmly grazing camel seems well aware of this as it unhurriedly chews the vegetation. This is a safe place of respite for all. I am reminded that most dreaming contains a safe place somewhere around. If I were working Ngintaka's dreaming, I'm sure this is the place where I would start, before entering the cave of paranoia. The landscape is becoming a dream practicum.

From the hillside, rocks protrude. A horizontal rock bows like a lean-to over an oblong triangle lying on its back. These are Ngintaka's rust-red chin and beard. Here he stopped and turned to stone. Around these hills he had gone hunting and caught his prey. Now, lounging around after dinner, he cleans bits of meat from his beard and muses, "Oh, what a handsome fellow I am!"

What a delight, that landscape can be vain! We recognize ourselves, and laugh. I clap along with the Pitjantjatjara song enthusiastically. Vanity is an element of the wild. It is not just me, sinful old me.

"The creation story is in the land to teach the people," Nganyinytja explains. I understand. "Along the song line," she continues, "different peoples have the responsibility for the songs in their place, to keep them alive in the land. This here is the song line of my family, the Pitjantjatjara side, from this point to where Ngintaka dies." The movement of her arms is sweeping and elegant as she gestures toward the expanse of her land. "Down further south, where Ngintaka stole the grindstone, is the land of the Yankunytjatjara people. It is their responsibility to keep the land there alive with song. And then it goes over to the next people, and then the next. This keeps the country alive."

She doesn't mean that the various people keep a story or a tradition alive. They keep *the country* alive with their song. The country is a living being that has to be nurtured with song and dance. I understand now why dreams of song and dance are commonly the ones ordinary Pitjantjatjara remember. Those dreams revitalize the cosmos. They have to be remembered and taught, in order to fuse with the dreaming of a people.

At a point where the mountains are slightly higher the desert car stops. We are led to a long spine of odd, gray-ocher boulders with marks perfectly round, as though they were burnt in by humans. Yet they couldn't be. They look strikingly like the skin of a *Perentie* lizard: Ngintaka.

"These rocks are only found in this small corridor up here," Diana, in her Australian accent explains Nganyinytja's words. "Here Ngintaka gets nauseous. He dances around and then he vomits. He vomits out the seeds of mistletoe berries. He is responsible for other seeds as well. Grass seeds. He vomits those elsewhere. That's why they have the marking of his skin. These are the seeds of the fruit he had eaten."

Nganyinytja points to a large stone with striking *Perentie*-skin markings, and a place where the markings have clearly been rubbed with another stone. "Nganyinytja's father took her here as a little girl," Diana tells me, "to show her how to grind this marked stone with a small rock. That has to be done every spring before the rain comes to insure a lot of mistletoe berries." I am surprised that the stones that look like lizard skin are seeds, not Ngintaka himself. It seems that the seeds have become part of him. All the seeds the people use have first been inside Ngintaka. His dreaming pervades them. Each seed has its place in the Ngintaka order of being.

The women dance the vomit dance. They make little jumps, and while their arms swing like pendulums, they rhythmically stretch and bend the fingers of their open hands, portraying a sowing motion. This recalls the way Ngintaka threw out the seeds. It is a woman's dance. My wife and daughter find it humorous that the one dance they learn in the Center is the vomit dance.

A long stone farther down the path is Ngintaka's tail, next to what clearly looks like his footprint. Appearances in the landscape are consistent with the stories. I'm not surprised that a group of boulders turns out to be wild onions, Ngintaka-style.

Finally, we reach the high point of our journey: we will enter the empty belly of Ngintaka. They point out the cave in a boulderlike rockface. We climb up and enter.

I'm taken aback. This is obviously the mouth of Ngintaka. You can see his glottis hanging down. The far

end of the grotto is painted with symbols that tell the
story. The most recent markings are by Nganyinytja and
Ilyatjari's son. It appears that each generation paints it
anew.

Six-year-old Christopher gathers little branches together. In the empty belly of Ngintaka we have to light a
fire. With the light coming in from a chimneylike shaft
above us, we can conduct a speleology of Ngintaka. Here
is the empty belly, after the vomit but before death. . . .
Ngintaka is to die farther down. Is this hunger, craving,
emptiness? What agony is he going through? We climb up
through his belly to find a spectacular view of the desert
floor below. The rains have greened the landscape. I
breathe deep, coming out from inside the lizard.

When we get back to the camp we'r tired. Diana
makes tea and tells of a woman who got ɔ nauseous on
the Ngintaka trail tnat she had to ɔ back to Alice
Springs. I smile benevolently about so much hysterical
identification. We go to bed early. I dream.

**I am with a group wanting to understand the dreaming.
There seems to be an old group and a new group. I join the
old group and become terribly nauseous. I remember the
vomiting dreaming of Ngintaka. Also the vomiting dance.**

I wake up and scramble out of my sleeping bag in order
not to vomit all over it. I feel sick as hell. I realize that I
am still in symbiosis with Ngintaka. Or maybe I am sick
because I chose the old order instead of joining the new:
preferring the old white order of Jung in the barber's chair
over the dark voice of the wild.

The nausea recedes. I look up and see the clouds above
me. A gigantic eagle with a wingspan crossing the entire

sky flies overhead. After a few seconds of observation it disappears. Nothing in the sky looks even remotely like the bird shape I just saw. Then there is a flash of lightning and it begins to drizzle. I get up to cover our belongings.

This is our last night in the bush. I don't fall asleep after this. It begins to rain and I hear the Aboriginal camp stir. They seem in the process of leaving, getting into the car. I hear them shout at the children, then drive off. I miss them intensely. I still wanted to speak to Ilyatjari, to tell him about my understanding of the dreaming. That the vomiting lives in the land and that when confronted with the place, the nausea *is* the dreaming. The nausea belongs to the spirit of the place.

Thank God, they come back. I am very relieved. I go up to them to tell them about my dream and to give Ilyatjari my book *Dreaming with an AIDS Patient*. His son Jonathan can read English. For some reason I want Ilyatjari to know the AIDS dreaming.

When I tell him about the eagle, he says, "Very strong spirit." He asks if I could see the back of the neck, since the ngankari keeps his own head. I say no. He grins and begins to cough terribly. He has severe emphysema. I feel very warmly toward him. Had this meeting with white-haired Ilyatjari the eagle-man been a catalyst for a reemergence of my father in the dreams I had in the out-back and later on?

When we leave, he asks me to come back and bring other ngankaris like myself.

Worlds apart, we are colleagues.

CHAPTER 6

Dream Practicum 1: Change of Season

[Flashback to the July summer a few weeks before my August winter in Australia. A change of season in my life is about to take place, as it is for the woman who presents her dream to us in the boiling-hot room at the Omega Institute in upstate New York. The following report is a reconstruction based on an audiotaped session.]

IT IS ONE OF THE HOTTEST DAYS IN MEMORY AND THEY'VE LOCATED our practicum for dreamworkers, therapists, and other lovers of dreams, in a room that is fully exposed to the sun. We started out with too many participants, thirty-eight, but the heat has reduced it to twenty-four, a manageable amount. We're dying of heat—a woman announces that she has had a dream about ice the night before. Hoping for cooling, we take her dream as our material.

I have met her before and know that she is recuperating from a very serious illness that had taken a chunk of several years out of her life. She had written to me about the illness, chronic fatigue syndrome, and told me that lately she has felt its grip beginning to loosen, making it possible for her to experience more active time in her day.

We listen to the dream as it is told to us in the present tense. It will be told twice, so we can listen the first time with half an ear—and with an ear-and-a-half to our own responses.

"I'm walking on a street, on a sidewalk," she begins. A shiver goes up my spine, from my tailbone up. Then I feel cold and nauseous.

> There are big concrete squares; there are lines on the sidewalk. On my left there is a park; it is very shady. It's a city park, like Central Park, but not quite that citylike. It's a big park. On my right there is a street. It is down below, on a bank, with a big curb up from the street. And it is early spring or late winter. I'm mostly aware of the ice and the water in the street on my right. There are rocks of ice, kind of breaking up, almost like a river, and water flowing down the street. It is melting ice. I'm walking along the sidewalk and my dog comes up from across the street. And I'm a little concerned, but she is very careful. She comes up to me and we go into my truck, which is at the end of the sidewalk in the street. The street curves around and there is a fork or something at the end of the walk. And then we get into my car and drive off.

"And that is the end of the dream?"

"Yep," she replies, upbeat.

A pang of distant panic comes with the feeling of not knowing what the hell to do with this dream. I have this feeling every time I work with a dream, but every time I am tricked out of routine defenses against this horrible uncertainty by the conviction that, although at other times something did come out of the dreamwork, *this* time really nothing will emerge. Not-knowing has a way of seeping in through the cracks of my insecurity.

For a moment I'm annoyed with myself, wondering why I expose myself to these unpleasant, insecure feelings. Why in God's name do I work with dreams! All I can do is wait until it passes, this initiatory panic at the entrance of dreaming.

While waiting, I review my bodily reactions to the dream. There had been a shiver in the beginning accompanied by a sensation of being cold. And then I became nauseous. I have no idea what it means. I am just noticing things about myself that are going on. My attention is drawn to this shiver because I felt it before she talked about the ice, as though my body received the atmosphere of the dreaming a moment before it was verbalized. At that point I must have been close to the dreaming.

Judging from the intensity of my physical response, there may be a great deal of turmoil present in the "atmosphere" of the ice. I'd better not begin there. Suddenly, my terror of the unknown has taken a backseat as I prepare for the wilderness expedition. All systems are put on alert.

It is not necessary to start working on a dream at the beginning of the narrative. I am more interested in the wildlife existing *alongside* the narrative. The "story" of the dream as told by the waking ego stems from a thin band of consciousness: a grave limitation, considering the fact that it is only one among other forms of consciousness of which the totality of the dreaming consists. It is like listening exclusively to one single station on the AM band, when you know that there are many different stations emitting consciousness on several different frequencies.

So I will not start this dream at the beginning, after

having this strong experience around ice, the breaking of the ice, and the icy street. In this case, I want to work the dream backward, starting in dog-land before facing the ice. I will start with the dog and the feelings related to the dog, who seems to be a close familiar to the dreamer. Dogs are loyal helpers in protecting safe places, and we could use a safety in case we stumble upon something frightful. The ice-scape could be frightening. I'd rather have help before diving into emotional deep freeze.

"When do you first see the dog," I ask, "and where do you see her? By the way, is it a she-dog?"

"Yes. When I first see her, she is crossing. She is real close to the edge of the bank, but she is still crossing the road. That is actually the scariest point in the dream for me. The place where I'm most frightened. I feel intense fear in my chest."

I turn to the group, which I have meticulously kept abreast of each fluctuation of my interior process—this being a practicum—in an attempt to connect them with the inner life of dreamwork. "So you see, all my strategizing appears totally wrong. I believed the dog-place would be a safe spot for starters. . . . It doesn't matter." Laughter. I grin sheepishly. Like a weathervane, I let myself be blown in any direction.

"So what is going on in your chest as the dog comes up?"

"When she comes up I'm really scared that she is going to get hit by a car. It's a busy street, and she is coming through these cars. I'm afraid for her."

I notice that she has stopped breathing. I pause while she continues to hold her breath in fear. I wait for this psychophysical experience of fear to engrave itself upon her memory. The relationship between fear and breath is

lodged in her chest: intensification of focus creates awareness in the chest. The bodily experience of the fearing
chest emerges into consciousness.

When I feel the fearful-chest awareness has sunk in, I
relax. "Keep breathing and stay with your dream." Now I
weave back to waking life, throwing a line to the shores of
the familiar in a two-way motion: exporting dream life to
waking consciousness and importing waking familiarity
into dreaming. "Is this a fear you know?"

"Yeah. I just left her this weekend for the first time in a
long time. But it is a familiar fear."

"Is it a feeling that you are going to lose her?"

"Not so much that I'm going to lose her, but that she
will die. She is twelve years old and I've had her the whole
time."

"And is she a very close friend?"

"Yes, she's one of my best friends."

There is a silent moment while she feels the proximity
of death and loss. An emotional density hangs in the
room. We can all feel the atmosphere of death and loneliness that seems to be the climate in this territory. It feels
as though we've dropped into a valley that is moist, like a
vale of tears. It pulls us down farther. I feel the force of the
pull.

"Let's move on a little bit more," I suggest, "so we can
get deeper into the image. We're in an emotional down-
draft. Let's see what happens next."

"She's not afraid at all. She is very relaxed and her
mouth is open and smiling and she's panting. She has
really good timing, coming through these cars and coming
through the water. She's sort of slopping her way up to
the bank."

"Is it icy there or not?" I ask, in order to introduce the frozen hinterlands of soul.

"It is icy in the street, but not so much when she comes up the bank. It is still moist. It is wet. But the ice is in the street. She is sort of walking along. She is very graceful and sort of deliberate. But there is nothing anxious about her gait at all. She is sort of having a good time, hangin' out, wading her way through the water and coming towards me."

"You say her tongue is hanging out of her mouth?" I want to feel the interior sense of the dog's motion, the dog's experience of the surrounding reality. Since the most sensitive spot related to the dog's experience is in the dreamer's chest—where she felt pain and held her breath when she felt the loss of the dog—I attempt to transit into the dog by way of breathing.

"Her mouth is open. Her tongue isn't way out of her mouth. She has this smiley, relaxed expression. Her tongue isn't past the end of her mouth. It is sort of just hangin' out there."

"Can you notice how she is breathing?"

"She is just breathing very, very regularly. More quickly than I am breathing, but very regularly for her."

"Can you feel her breathing?" I notice that my voice drops almost to a concentrated whisper, very audible and intensely soft.

"Uh-huh." She nods, feeling dog-breathing.

"Her tongue?"

"Uh-huh," she utters, feeling dog-tongue.

"How does that feel, that breathing and her tongue?"

"Pretty happy-go-lucky. It's loose in her mouth. There isn't a lot of deliberateness to any of it."

"As she is moving through traffic, what is going on inside her? Try and feel her breathing and her mouth as she is moving through traffic."

"She is in a flow. Not sort of consciously, but serendipitously in a flow with her own movements and with the traffic so that nothing is hitting her. She comes really close at one point to the front wheels of a car, but she just comes right through before it crunches her." The fluidity of the dog-friend can be felt by all.

"So she is not frightened?"

"No. She knows just where she is going. It doesn't even feel like a matter of choice. She is just in the timing."

"How does it feel to be in the timing?"

"Loose, very loose. Very graceful. I feel my body, I feel the inside of my skin, I feel the weight of my body, the heat of it, the temperature of it, and a sort of looseness."

"What are you feeling in your spine?" I inquire, as I feel an ache around the small of my back, one of my sensitive spots (aka a bad back). This ache hadn't been around a moment ago, so I wonder if our symptoms correspond.

"It's loose. I couldn't sit rigidly upright if I wanted to. There is one spot in my spine, where those two little dots are in the back. Below the small of the back. A little bit above them there's one tight vertebra."

I thank my good fortune that I have run into a dreamer with a detailed, inner awareness of her body. Some people with a serious physical illness have developed this detailed inner sense in order to navigate through the dangerous terrain of malady.

"Was that tight vertebra already there?"

"No, it feels like it's connected to her."

"Can you feel yourself into that spot? What are you feeling there?"

"An old wound."

"What kind of an old wound?"

"The image that came up spontaneously is a memory. When I found her she was beaten up. She had been shot in the leg." She pauses. "I feel a connection between that spot in my spine, the inside of my thigh where her wound is, and my right knee where I had a whole surgical adventure. I can feel the connection through those three spots."

"Can you stay with the connection between those three spots? Concentrate on them. What are you feeling?" I insist, enjoying her sensitivity. She's a good interior observer.

"The spot in the back feels like the place where there is the most emotion in connection with the other two. I feel an energy current, but it doesn't have just to do with grief, and it's older. This feeling around my dog is the current manifestation of older feelings. It has been around forever, for as long as I remember, this pain in my back. The feelings are much older."

I turn to the group for a short explanation, a time-out.

"The reason why I went to the spine was because I felt something down here." I point to my lower back. "That's why I would now go on with that spot, because it is something that absolutely corresponds between the dreamer and myself. If I had felt a symptom in my knee, I might go on with the knee. But since I have the same thing happening with my back as the dreamer does, a sensation that wasn't there beforehand, I continue with the small of the back."

I turn to the dreamer. "You say it's an old ache that lives there?"

"It might be. It feels old and new. Future, past, and present."

"Can you concentrate on that spot and bring all your focus there?" I suggest.

We can feel the concentration intensify.

"Now it opens up and travels up the left side of my spine. I can feel a connection between that spot and a spot in my shoulder right here," she says, patting her shoulder blade. "But there is less emotion in this top spot."

I feel that energy has begun to circulate. I turn to the group again.

"Now we have followed some of the emotions through the body and it is time to go back into the dream." Shifting back to the dreamer: "Does the dog walk towards you or is she running?"

"She is sort of just walking through the road, and then when she gets to the bank she goes a little more quickly, 'cause it's a little steep and she needs a little momentum to get up the bank. It's just the amount of momentum necessary to go up the bank, nothing extra. She's not hurried in any way. Then she just falls into pace beside me. I think I pat her head, I am really glad to see her. I feel deep relief and gratitude that she is okay."

"Because at the moment she was just in front of the wheel you were very frightened," I remind her.

"I can feel that in my throat," she responds. "It comes up like a clutching. If my throat were a fist it would be going from an open hand to not quite a clenched fist, but a kind of claw almost. I feel tension in the hand. Fear. The fear and the grief go together. Part of the fear, I think, is a feeling of grief. They are separate but also connecting."

She stops. An association distracts her attention. I wait.

"It's all this twin stuff. I was conceived as a twin and my twin miscarried two months into my mother's pregnancy with me. As if I remember this dying on a cellular level. I feel that kind of emotion again, as well as the immediate feelings about the dog dying."

We're all silent, feeling death—our own, our beloveds'.

"Can you feel how we are on a deeper level now?" I ask the group. Moving down into the dreaming is like descending through an ever denser atmosphere. At first the images are flimsy and unstable, volatile like vapors. Then the images begin to solidify, becoming more substantial. At present we have entered into this visceral presence of the dreaming.

I turn back to the dreamer. "Can you go to the moment where your hand is on the head of your dog?"

"Yes, both hands. I sort of bend down and cup her face. I just love her. I'm really glad she's okay. This fear I feel is both of her pain and of my loss. The fear of her pain if she gets physically hurt and mine of losing her. I fear both."

"What do your hands feel?"

"Very soft. I feel the warmth of her body. Her face is so familiar to my hands. My hands are very relaxed."

"Can you let that sense of relaxed familiarity go through your body?"

"It does, it flows right through me. My back completely changes, so do my legs. It just flows right through."

From the familiar dog the familiarity transfers into her introspective body. Now that she experiences this familiarity, relaxation, and safety in her senses, in her body, we can go to the element of the dream where soul shivers. I pause before the transition. At this point there are several choices. We could go back to the death-of-the-wombmate experience, feel that again and experience the fear and loss in that image. I am sure, however, that she has gone over this image so many times that it feels kind of stale. I have a preference for fresh material, and opt to go directly to the ice.

"When you first remember—when the memory of the dream begins—where are you?"

"I just have a really strong hit of this park, it could be a graveyard. The park on the left is sort of Central Park, but it could also be a graveyard. I am on this sidewalk."

Of course, the graveyard motif is seductive after all these feelings of death, so it could be a distraction. I'm after the ice. I check. "And the part you see that could be a graveyard, is that the place where you see the ice?"

"No, the ice is down the street on the right. The park is on the left. If there is a graveyard, it is up forward and to the left. It is the direction I am walking in, but I don't see the gravestones from here." I'm glad I checked. "I just see this tree-lined park. It is a little dark; not exactly dark, but shaded. The street is full of ice."

"Can you concentrate on the ice?" I encourage. "What does the ice look like?"

"Big blocks. It's grayish, bluish, whitish. Really big blocks of ice. It looks like a river. There are all these images of blocks of ice melting and moving. And the water is flowing over them. It looks like a frozen river breaking up, but it is more symmetrical. It really *is* in the street. Odd shapes, sort of triangular. They fit together. They have substance to them."

The merging of the image of the pedestrian street with a primal undercurrent indicates we're moving toward a fundamental experience, deep in the wilderness where pedestrian individual experience meets melting ice ages populating the soul of each of us. In the deep wilderness, the individual experience fuses with wild, preindividual experiences *anyone* could have. Jung calls these preindividual,

untamed forces *archetypal*, existing in *collective* unconscious-
ness.

"Feel the cold." I notice the imperative in my voice. I'm
apparently increasing the pressure.

"Right now I feel surrounded by the ice. I have moved
to the edge of the bank. There are big blocks of ice
around me and I can feel the coldness radiating off them
and cooling me. But I can feel the temperature change
from the sidewalk to the edge of this ice block."

"What is the quality of the cold?"

"From this distance? From this distance it is cool. I can
feel it penetrating my skin. It's a really concentrated cold.
It's not in my bones, but it's ice-cold. The water is less
scary than the ice. The water is really cold, but the ice has
the kind of feeling of when you put an ice cube to your lip
and it sticks to your lip. The ice has that kind of feeling.
Uh-oh!" Her exclamation conveys fear.

"You have to try and go very slowly. Approach the ice
and water very slowly, otherwise we will run into a solid
wall of fear." She nods. "The ice is in motion, you said?" I
direct her attention to a more distant view of the ice, a
viewpoint from which patterns can be seen. It leads her
away from the direct, frozen fear. Respite.

"My impression is of ice in real movement. There seems
to be a change of season."

"Can you feel that change of season in your body?"

She cries softly. "I'm afraid." Her voice trembles behind
her tears. "Everything is moving. I'm afraid of getting overwhelmed by the water flow that is created when the ice
breaks up. This is a new season and it comes in with the
power of ice melting and of water carrying the ice down
in a movement that is very elemental."

I imagine how her body is coming out of the winter of

her chronic fatigue syndrome. The rigid status quo of her illness, freezing her into sixteen hours of inactivity per day, is cracking. The river of life is beginning to flow once more. No wonder she is frightened of drowning, of being swept away by the season of renewal.

"How does it feel in your body, this elemental movement of the ice?" We are now in primordial wilderness, where the elements reign.

"I have this attraction-repulsion. There is energy coming up through my body and also the fear of being overwhelmed by that energy. I'm afraid I won't know how to contain it without breaking up myself. My dog negotiates the breakup of the ice really easily. She just comes right through that flow of the ice." The last sentence has an undertone of puzzlement. The spontaneous emergence of the familiar dog who can manage the new season may be helpful.

"Keep the dog close. Keep that feeling of your dog close as you begin to feel that overwhelming flow coming in. Keep the dog close to you, the sense of the dog."

I turn to the group, a proud tone of vindication in my voice. "Time-out. Now you can see that it was good to get the sense of the dog first and only then go to the ice." I turn back to the dreamer.

"What are you feeling right now?"

"How invigorating it is. I just felt a wave of physical invigoration. I didn't just feel the flow, but the coldness of the water at the same time. That cold flow of water is invigorating. It is very different from the coldness of the ice. That icy season feels very familiar to my body. I feel like I've spent a lot of time there. Something about touching the ice scares me. I'm afraid my skin will stick to it. That I'll never be free. The ice frightens me."

"How does the fear of the ice feel in your body?"

"In my chest I can feel it. Not so much like a weight, but like a body, like a little body." She is now very emotional and repeats the last sentence several times. She points to her chest. "Right here. It's like this body was stuck in my chest."

"How big is this little body?"

"It's every size. From the size of a sweet pea to the size of one of those Russian dolls you can take apart and then there is a smaller doll inside."

"And can you feel how this tiny being lives in your chest?"

"It is more the memory of it that is left behind in my chest. I feel the impression of it here, like something has been gripping your arm, and you let go and you still feel the impression. But the substance of it, the being itself, is now in my belly. I want to stay with the impression in my chest where it seemed to be. When I feel the impression the being left behind in my chest, it helps it move down. It's like saying good-bye to this little being in my chest. It has always been there in my chest. It is frightening that it is no longer there. That it has dropped down. It feels new. I'm scared. I'm afraid to feel it down in my belly. The icy season and the body in my chest belong together. I love them. They're so familiar. It is hard to leave them behind. It's a sense of grieving and of good-bye. Now I can go down to my belly."

Here is the direct experience of the difficulty of leaving the status quo behind, however painful this state may be: this little self-of-the-icy-season living in her chest was at least familiar. It goes *way* back, even provoking a sense of prenatal memories. Every long-term illness or neurosis left behind has to be grieved over, as we leave behind a self we have been on very close terms with. However much suffering it has caused us, we still miss it, because we knew it well.

"What does it feel like down in your belly?"

"Very soft. A bed of blood, soft and rich. Like a bed of blood and nourishment. It's very red."

We have dropped into a womb of springtime. I give us time to feel the season of renewal, the rebirth after a season of death. Then I move on toward the contrast between winter and spring. She is right between the two. Winter is no longer, spring not yet.

"Just stay with that feeling in your body and get back to the feeling of the ice. Keep concentrating on your belly and feel the ice on your skin. How is it different, the ice-cold touch and the feeling in your belly?"

"My right hand is on my belly, and with my left hand I can really lean on the ice."

"Can you feel the difference between your right hand and your left hand?"

"Yeah, very much," she exclaims, surprised. "My right hand is very warm and my left hand is very cold. All the cold is coming in from the left and all the warmth is circulating from the right. Now they are beginning to sort of merge. Can you feel that too?" Apparently she feels very connected to me at this moment, convinced I am feeling the same as she does. And, strangely enough, I do. I feel the merging of the warmth and the cold.

"Uh-huh," I concur.

"There is a hand-shaped impression in this piece of ice now. As the warmth starts to touch the ice it melts it in the shape of my hand."

"Now stay with this and feel how it develops. We will

stop the work here and you keep on going from here by yourself."

"I can do that."

"Breathe into it. Breathe down into the point where the warmth and the cold begin to merge. In that way you'll stay connected to it," I suggest. The dreamwork has set a process in motion. It is now the dreamer's task to stay connected to it. She now has the experience of the melting ice at her fingertips.

I started presenting dream practica in the late seventies, to demonstrate, in the most direct fashion I knew, my ways of working with dreams. The purpose was entirely didactic. What I had not counted on was the profound cathartic effect dreamwork has on participants of the practicum who are not presenting their own dream. As in Greek tragedy, the observers go through a catharsis while experiencing the fate of the protagonist. Collective elements from the wilderness of preindividual dreaming begin to reverberate in all of us, like the melting of the ice with the dog dreamer at this present practicum. Not only is her body numbed by the deep freeze of her chronic fatigue syndrome, she's also frozen stiff by fears of change, by a dread of life's fundamental unpredictability. It is part of being human to have these fears. Dreamwork gives all participants a most acute experience of the human condition. No life-insurance policy can save us from the permanent imminence of change.

[My dream series in Australia illustrates this reality. In this series of dreams, beginning the night I first slept in Australia, several themes return with regularity, like the pain around the death of my father. The theme of *constant change* was another motif. I dream:

I'm going into the outback. There is a group. It is known that the most important experiences are in the dark, in the unknown. Then there is someone who heads up another group and he just breaks into the unknown, a world of constant change.]

Besides the cathartic experience of practicum participants —because their own depths begin to resonate—it became apparent that a group can approach a dream from a broader spectrum of perspectives than an individual dreamworker can. Things that did not occur to me to ask were asked by participants in the practicum, adding several extra layers to the work. Similarly, the focus of a concentrated group on a single dream for a long period of time led to depths previously inaccessible to me in individual work. Of course, the trust level in one-to-one psychoanalysis is usually so much higher than it is in groupwork that an intimate atmosphere not encountered in groups is established. This leads to other kinds of depths inaccessible through group work. Yet I found group dreamwork, as one manner of entering the dreamworld to lead to surprising results.

This led to the formation of small dream groups. These groups are for people not necessarily interested in therapy, but who want to quicken their sense of existence by a deep immersion in dreaming. An ideal *dreamwork group*, consisting of four to six people, meets once a week for two and a half to three hours. As an overture, half an hour is used to talk about general topics around dreaming and to discuss the previous session. Participants ask the previous week's dreamer for a follow-up. The dreamer tells what kind of aftereffects the work has had during the week: moods, dreams, and interactions that were reminiscent of dream motifs. The dog dreamer, for example, could tell the group if the dreamwork had influenced her feelings toward her illness and her recovery. She would be asked if new insights had emerged. What is said most frequently by people who have worked on their dreams in the group is that the mood has stayed around for some time after the work. This overture period of the group session is also used to reflect on, among other things, the way the work was conducted and techniques that were used. After this the group tries to locate the dream that most urgently wants to be presented. Everyone who wants to report a dream does so. A dream is selected. (Short dreams are generally easier to contain in groups, especially in groups that are just starting out.) Usually it is obvious who needs to work and the selection is spontaneous: other dreamers defer. The actual dreamwork, up to two hours, is the centerpiece of the session. Finally, the group tends to close with a wrap-up period of twenty minutes for processing the work that's just been done.

When meeting once a week, it is thus possible for each member of the group to have one of her or his dreams worked upon every four to six weeks. This frequency, though it seems sporadic, is actually quite sufficient, because of the dramatic effects dreamwork has on participants while working on other people's material. In our surface-oriented society, participating in-depth in another's life is generally experienced as a rare privilege by members of the group.

A dreamwork group needs *leadership*. This leadership can, however, be a *function* that rotates among the members. The leader of a dreamwork group basically functions much as the conductor of an orchestra, keeping the music playing in the right tempo and atmosphere.

The dream is told twice. The first time, participants focus on their own experiences while listening to the dream. After this first telling, those who have felt fluctuations of attention, changes in body sensations, and other distractions that might be related to the dream in some way or other remark briefly on what they have experienced. These responses might be used as tools for the work ahead; they also free the listener to concentrate on the content of the dream during the second telling.

After the second telling it is the leader's task to keep the questioning process going, to keep it geared toward making the dreamer *reenter* the dream as deeply as possible, and help the group steer clear of questions that feel interpretative. When a group functions optimally, the dreamer hardly notices who asks the questions: they seem to come from a single organism.

There are, however, moments when several trails might be followed and group members veer off into conflicting directions, often leading to an ugly cacophony. The group stops producing a harmonic line of investigation. The dreamer begins to feel *uncontained* by the group, as if the group were a sieve, rather than a vessel sturdy enough to pour emotions into. At this point the leader takes over by calling "Time-out!"—the signal for a discussion of the work in progress. (Each group member, including the dreamer, may call for a time-out, but the leader is obliged to do so, since it is her or his *primary task to protect the dreamer.*) The group then focuses on one line of inquiry.

At moments when a certain intimacy of emotion on the part of the dreamer requires that he or she be addressed in a single voice, in order not to break the concentration, the leader takes over if no one else wants to speak. At these times, the group supports the dreamwork process by staying silently focused. Their silent active attention helps to keep the process concentrated.

Finally, like a conductor, the leader is responsible for pacing the work so that it will go deep *and* will fit within the alloted time frame. Usually, *the slower the work can be conducted, the more energy it takes to remain focused, the deeper it penetrates into the unknown.*

Thus, much of dreamwork is spent *waiting*. If we don't wait on images, we often start imposing our wishes and expectations on situations. By *slowing down*, and careful observation, we learn to differentiate between ego expectations and authentic imagination. The woman at the bar who showed the picture of her family to the man on the bar stool next to her was sure that he was going to disapprove of her, while in fact he felt a friendly curiosity toward her. In the dreamwork, had we moved to this image quickly, with the question, "What do you suppose the man thinks about you?" she might have experienced him as rejecting.

By transiting into a dream-other through a slow process of careful observation, empathy, and eventual identification, it is possible to feel the reality of that dream-other from within. This gives both dreamworker and dreamer a strong sense of the *authenticity* of the dream-other. He appears not as someone who was *invented* by the dreamer but as an organic entity *presenting itself to* the dreamer.

A good way to enhance a tolerance for waiting is by concentrating on *breathing*. Whether you are a dreamworker or dreamer—or both, working on your own dream—notice how your breath moves through your body, and how it changes at various moments during the work. This keeps you connected to a physical consciousness, expanding your awareness beyond the narrow confines of the head. It can also be very helpful during moments of panic and anxiety. The dreamer should be encouraged to stay with what she is feeling and to simultaneously concentrate on the breathing body. Often the suggestion to breathe down into the feet, leading to a heightened sense of connection between feet and ground, can provide a necessary, literally grounding experience, when the dreamer feels she will explode all over the map. By calming down this way, the dreamer can experience the frightening emotions without giving in to the strong urge to repress them.

Because he started as a hypnotist, Sigmund Freud began dreamwork—in the context of psychoanalysis—by *immobilizing the dreamer* on a couch. He employed physical stillness to reach the deepest levels of memory. (When Freud coined the hyphenated word *dream-work* he was referring to the unconscious process that produces manifest dream-material from latent dream-thoughts. Our use of the unhyphenated word *dreamwork* describes the craft that employs dreams as its material.) *Sitting still* continues to be an invaluable tool for dreamwork. I have been told that the great tenor Luciano Pavarotti, when singing in a nonoperatic context, holds a white handkerchief in his hand: when the handkerchief hangs absolutely still, he knows that all his energy is focused in his voice and nothing trails off into unnecessary body movement. Besides the powerful focus created by inhibiting motion, stillness also provides an opportunity to concentrate on subtle impulses, on exploring an image before the impulses aroused by the image erupt into action. By inhibiting action, tension rises. In working our dreams, alone or with others, we are often bursting with a desire to move, to do something. But at such a moment, not doing anything may make *insights* burst forth, with full visceral impact.

On the other hand, when—because—the norm is not to move, movements may have significant impact. Sometimes, experiencing a *body movement* that arises from an image can lead to subtle insights. Imitating the movement of a dream figure may be helpful in getting a sharper sense of his or her reality. Moving around the room in the way of the insecure President Clinton in the White House dream may reveal his inner life.

It is usually helpful if the participants in the dream groups are relative strangers who don't have a primary tie to each other. People tend to talk more easily to strangers; in addition, the occasional "acting out" (that is, acting toward a participant in the group with the psychological force intended for a dream person) is thus limited to the period during which the group has actual contact. I usually notify participants who are in primary relationships that fallout from the dream group might occur in their relationship, and that they should be vigilant.

This is not the only danger of dreamwork. *The greatest danger when working on dreams in groups is provoking shame and embarrassment.*

When a person presents a dream, he has no idea where the dreamwork will lead. Often, very intimate confessions arise spontaneously. Sometimes these revelations may embarrass the dreamer to the point where he feels burdened afterward with unbearable shame. In dreamwork most heat is generated by the most intimate experiences. It is easier for a dreamer to talk about the elemental essence of ice-cold fear—a feeling anyone could have—than to talk, say, about sexual frigidity, something that is felt to be much more intimate. (I am not referring to the dog dreamer. This is just an example.) The more intimate the material a group works on, the more pressure is applied on the capacity of the group to contain this volatile material. As a rule, the alchemists say that *the strength of the vessel has to be proportionate to the tension in the material,* otherwise the vessel explodes. Especially during the beginning period of a dream group, the strength of the group *as a group* is, at times, not up to the heat generated by the work. This can give rise to uncontained moments ending in profound feelings of shame in the dreamer. Shame is a dangerous, sometimes lethal, emotion. It should not be provoked! It accompanies the experience of exposure. Overexposure may lead to unbearable shame.

To avoid this, we often *work in the blind.* When asking for an association, when one suspects that a very intimate experience is involved, the participants can ask the dreamer to focus on an association without telling the group. After the dreamer has thoroughly felt the impact of this association—often, for instance, a painful childhood memory one feels embarrassed about—the group has the dreamer return to the dream, while feeling the emotions this memory brought about. In this way, the feeling tone of the association can be imported without the dreamer experiencing possibly destructive, false crosswinds of shame and embarrassment toward the group. The leader, in order to protect the dreamer, sees to it that work that could cause unmanageable embarrassment out in the open is switched to work in the blind.

The members of the group have to help the dreamer retain a sense of dignity, even in the most undignified situations. As a group has been together longer, working in the blind happens less and less.

Dreamwork has its dangers. Therefore, as a rule, it is agreed that *everyone enters at their own risk.*

Often, at the beginning of dreamwork, someone announces that they never dream. Upon further probing it is frequently revealed that the person actually has dreams; they just don't conform to the person's criteria for what a dream is supposed to be. A "dream" is thought to be something special, certainly a narrative of some kind. Quite often, though, a dream floats to the surface of memory in the shape of an ordinary, single image: a woman standing by a door, a window in the kitchen, an ordinary moment at work, a man in a suit, a dark place, somewhere in a restaurant, crossing the street in traffic—something insignificant and boring.

We have a preference for narrative over image. We feel the more epic a dream is, the more significant it must be. Often, however, I find narrative *less* revealing than the single image, which, when truly entered into, yields great fruit. It is also common that, after working on such a dream snippet, other dreams follow.

Don't select your dreams before recording them. Resistances often make a dream seem trivial at first glance; after some mining work, these apparently insignificant dreams often yield a lot of material. Sometimes people don't write down those dreams that would be disapproved of by others (parents, spouse, suspected snoopers: "I always have the feeling that someone is peeking into my dream book when I'm not around"). Together with Saint Augustine, thank the higher powers who have made us not responsible for our dreams, and write down those dreams especially.

Never believe that you will remember this dream forever and therefore you don't have to write it down. After five minutes this "eternal" memory may have evaporated.

Sometimes, however, dreams *do* seem to be absent. At the least, some people remember fewer dreams than others. Dreamworkers can tend to have a dream-chauvinist attitude, insinuating that someone who remembers few dreams is somehow defective, that something is wrong. But there may be nothing wrong. Some people simply remember few or no dreams, for no particular reason, and that's that. A supposed defect presupposes a norm. Remembering dreams and not remembering dreams are equally normal. For people who do not remember dreams, dream groups are very helpful, because dreamwork makes the one who does not remember (in a way, that means all of us: we all forget 99 percent of our dreams) participate in dreaming.

For methods of *catching and recording* dreams, I have the laziness of repeating exercise 5, 6, and 7 of the first chapter on memory exercises in my *Little Course in Dreams:*

Observing the Moment of Awakening

Begin with the intention of waking up as consciously as possible. Try to really experience the transition between sleeping and waking. When you wake up, *before* your alarm goes off, remain exactly in the position you're in and observe the way sleeping transits to waking. Feel how your body wakes up. Where are the tensions? How does your head feel? Your breathing? And so on. Do this every day for a week and decide absolutely to remember *no dreams whatsoever.* The only thing that matters is observing the moment of waking.

Preparing to Record Your Dreams

After completing the week in the previous exercise, put a notepad and pen next to your bed. See to it that a *weak* light is within reach; it should be just strong enough to enable you to read your own handwriting. Or you could put a tape recorder next to your bed.

Now repeat the previous exercise, while at the same time being conscious that a writing pad or tape recorder is patiently waiting next to your bed. Try not to remember any dream. If one comes through anyway, record it.

Writing Down Your Dreams

1. You wake up with a shred of a dream that is still vaguely fluttering behind. Remain very quietly in the same position. Don't jump at the dream immediately, but look at it for a moment. Then, with closed eyes, grab the pen and write down exactly what you remember of this shred. Then stop again. Let your attention float alongside this image. Often another image of the same dream emerges. Write it down. From that point on you can often reel in the entire dream.

2. You wake up in the middle of the night with an entire dream and the feeling that there is so much to it you can't possibly write it all down. In that case, record the most salient details of the dream, with a few short descriptive words for a memory support. Then go back to sleep. If in the morning you haven't the foggiest idea what these code words refer to, it's gone wrong. In case you do remember, move through the images as through

specific spaces, and try to write down each detail more or less legibly. Many dreams disappear into illegibility.

3. You wake up in the morning with a dream. You begin writing down the last scene, and you write your way back to the beginning. Or just go from the beginning to the end. Don't dwell too much on the story line, or you might lose the details of the images. It is ideal to describe the images from *inside* them, so that you just have to look around.

In the shower and during breakfast you imprint the dream deeply into your memory. If you feel like it, you might tell it to someone. When you do, you often remember things that had remained outside your vision before. In telling the dream, there is already a mirroring taking place, without any comment from the other person. An outside ear changes the perspective. You learn the dream by heart as if it were a poem. The dream will start giving off words, like fragrances, as you muse about it. In this way you maintain access to your dreams throughout the day. Every time you go to the bathroom, or when you're alone for a moment, very briefly enter the dream. Remember each detail. Then, at night, just before you go to sleep, move through the dream once more.

Good night.

Saturday night in the muggy woods of upstate New York: we swat bugs and dream new dreams.

CHAPTER 7

Dream Practicum 2: Macabre Experiment

FRIDAY EVENING HE HAD COME UP TO ME AFTER THE FIRST SESSION of the dream practicum. He is a psychotherapist, with close-cropped hair and a kind, boyish face. Pushing forty, I'd say. He told me about his work with the AIDS plague, and we were instantly close to the point where I offered to come to his city to do HIV dreamwork with some of his patients. Ever since the experiences I wrote about in my book *Dreaming with an AIDS Patient*, this has been a matter very close to my heart.

On Saturday morning, while the dog dreamer experienced death and loss, he was sobbing quietly.

"When she was cupping the face of the dog," he tells us, after her dreamwork was ended, "I found myself feeling very much at one with her. It was like I was doing my own work."

"What was going on with you then?" I encourage him.

"My partner is dying. So that sense of imminent loss of somebody you love . . ." His voice trails off.

• • •

This buggy Saturday night, he has the startling dream he presents during our (audiotaped) Sunday morning session:

This dream has to do with the Addams family. Morticia and her husband are in their golf cart, which is a strange, boxy thing. Where there should be a place for their legs, there isn't. It's made out of real tacky brown Formica, or it might be covered plywood. It's very boxy. Not curvilinear at all. It moves with jerky movements. They are in line at the theater or a bank to get tickets, and I have the sense I am observing them from behind. I notice a woman who does a good job of masking her disdain or disgust.

In the second scene I am on the patio outside the garden of a woman with whom I've had a tryst the night before. On the left is a light stucco wall. Behind it is her house. On the wall are affixed crepe paper, or feather, dreamlike creations made by this Latin or Mediterranean woman who I made love with last night. She has made the mementos because she was so delighted with our time together. Some look like wings, and I associate dog-wings with that. The wings are in a small boutique bag. All of a sudden the Addams family is back on this patio with me. A donkey picks up the bag with the wings in it in its mouth and starts moving around. The donkey walks around in this area and I think there is no way of catching up with it. The donkey masticates on the handle. There is something fibrous in it which makes the donkey vomit. There is all this almost projectile vomit. Like white chunks of a very gelatinous material, or more dense than that. There is a stench. I reel from it. Morticia's daughter picks up one of these white chunks of vomit and I think, "What a bizarre child!" I had this sense of nausea just from the stench. That passes.

In the third scene there is the Addams family boy. He is

playing around with two hypodermic syringes he has clutched in his hand. One has the needle on it, the other one has the needle broken off. I manage to chase after him and to get the syringe, the one that does not have the needle, and force the fluid into his mouth. It is an anesthetic, which knocks him out. Using the other syringe I manage to get a little bit of the sedative into the girl, which slows her down. That's the end of the dream.

"Can you just tell us about the Addams family? Who are they?"

I am in the more or less advantageous position of never having seen *The Addams Family* on TV or in a movie theater, so I have few preconceptions. But even if it had been my favorite show and I'd seen each installment plus the feature movies, I'd still ask. My assumption is always that I don't know who public characters are *to the dreamer.*

"It's an occult family. They live in a haunted house. They're kind of a borderline family, in the sense that they live on the border between a normal existence and the other world. They have all these powers. . . . Strange creatures live in their house. There is always the sense of death hanging around them. Morticia is of a particularly ghoulish kind."

"Which aspect of death hangs around them?" I ask, as my desperate sense of disorientation before the abyss of unknowing recedes behind morbid curiosity.

"I'm not sure how to answer. There is no sense of immortality or some existence after death. Yet there is transcendence in this family. A ghostlike otherworldliness. They're not really the Addams family I know of the TV series from childhood. I really used to enjoy that. I've also seen the movie. But in the dream they don't have any particular association with either the TV or the movie. I just know that they are those characters."

"Can I mention an image I got when he was describing his dream?" a woman asks. I nod. She turns to the dreamer. "When you were talking about them in the golf cart getting tickets, I had a vision of the holocaust for some reason. It was very strong."

"I think it is relevant, this image of the holocaust," I remark. The group doesn't know his close relationship to AIDS. I had talked about it in private with the dreamer, so I don't know what I may reveal in public. I wait.

"My partner has AIDS," he tells us. "He's dying. And I work with AIDS all day long. Yes, that holocaust image is closely related to my world."

The mood in the room shifts perceptibly. Matters have become grave. Dreamwork on AIDS often begins in a leaden atmosphere, depressing, absorbed with the monstrosity of existence. If the alchemists are right in saying that the refined essence of poison is remedy, that each sickness carries its own cure in its heart—as we saw with the refrigerator dreamer whose confrontation with the essense of ice created a capacity for solitude—I wonder what we will find in the spirit of donkey vomit.

"Let's look at the golf cart," I decide, to get the process in motion. "Where are they? Are they in line at the bank?"

"The scene here is really quite vague. I have a sense that in the foreground there are the teller cages, but that's the only furniture. The rest is a spatial kind of thing. Some beginning piece of the dream was lost. I had this sense that the cart was moving with jerky movements. It moved the way it looked, without any curvilinear features you might expect of a vehicle. It was something like you might imagine with a very cheap stage production, nailing together a couple of cardboard boxes or something. Only it was substantive. It was made from this tacky brown-colored Formica. It has some kind of a projection in the front to accommodate their legs. There was a small projection, but it wasn't enough. But somehow they are in this thing. If they had legs, they wouldn't quite fit. So it's very puzzling."

"How is the cart able to move? Is someone pushing it?" someone asks.

"No. I had the sense it was motorized."

"Did it have wheels?" inquires another. The dreamgroup process steers the inquiry.

"I had the sense of that, although it is not really clear to me."

"Who is driving?"

"I can't remember his name. Morticia's husband."

"Where is the rest of the Addams family?"

"They're not there. There is just Morticia and Gomez. Now I remember his name."

Gomez feels incidental. Morticia seems to be the central person. "I have no idea what Morticia looks like," I remark, using my greencard alien status as a pretext for cultural innocence.

"She is really very thin. Gaunt, anorexic, long black hair, a dress that is so fitted to her body that she can't walk, because there is no space for her legs to move. It goes clear down to her ankles, so if she were to walk she could literally move her feet maybe an inch one from the other. Again, there is this sense of something unnatural about her. I have a sense that she is the one who is causing the stir here. Particularly with the woman who sees her. Morticia has outrageous makeup. She's dressed in black, but there is red somewhere in there as well. I'm not sure where it's coming from. Maybe Gomez is wearing red."

"Is she wearing red lipstick?" a woman wants to know.

"Yes. She's looking very witchlike with long nails painted black." Combinations of reds and blacks in the company of ghouls paint intimations of hell.

"Is she looking at you?" I ask.

"No. I don't have a sense of a dream ego at this point. I'm not in the dream. I am aware of a lot of tension and anxiety. A sense of tightness in my stomach. I have a sense that I am somewhat repelled by these people. I have the same response as the woman watching. I feel the dream from inside her."

"What does that repulsion feel like?"

"You could say that it is because of the way they look— very outrageous. But there is a deeper aspect, I think. It has to do with the aura of death that hangs about them. They live in a haunted house on the border between the world of the living and the world of the dead." He flinches. "I just had a real strong flash of feeling when I said 'the world of the living and the dead.' There was a tenseness throughout my body. I have a lot of trouble breathing—a sense of adrenaline rush and a lot of bottled-up tears. I could cry myself to exhaustion. Then it feels better for a while and then it happens again. But nothing really changes. I'm just as bottled up as ever."

"What associations do you have with the living dead?"

"There is some aspect of it that . . ." He fumbles, embarrassed.

"Just say it without any judgment," I encourage him.

"I sometimes feel that way when I'm with my partner now, because he's so physically wasted, so gone. He is already partly on the other side. I had actually flashed on an image of him looking worse than he does now. That image pops up now, out of the blue. It is very much like an image of the holocaust victims. I want to run," he exclaims. "I want to run away from him. I want to escape. I have this sense of incredible pent-up energy or tension. I'm having indigestion lately. I probably could battle it, but I don't. I know the indigestion is related to something that is not easy to stomach. But knowing that doesn't make it go away."

"What keeps you from running?" I press.

"Love. I know that he is my soul mate." He is deeply inside the ambivalence of love in extremis.

"Can you feel that in your body?"

"It's a big pressure right now."

I am reminded of the cupping of the dog's head, in the field between tenderness and loss. Yesterday he wept at this point. I pause, waiting for the right moment to transpose the work to a different key.

"Can you describe where you are with the donkey?" I ask after a long silence, in order to commence our move toward the point of the highest resistance. We transport his love pain to the donkey section, because in that section of the dream the sense of repulsion reaches its crescendo. In this move, some of the pressure diminishes. We give in a bit to his desire to run away from these feelings. Sometimes dreamwork is like catching large fish: the essential emotions are reeled in and then given slack; the fisherman is always aware that the line of connection must not break.

"We are in this patio area. Where the stucco wall ends there is a little gateway into a garden. The love mementos are on the wall. That's where the donkey got the shopping bag. The patio has an idyllic feeling to me, like southern

Italy or Greece. A stucco wall curves around to the front. It is quite high. I can't see over it. There is a small gate, a small opening, up there on the left, in the front where you can get the sense there's a little bit of a garden—grass, bushes, and maybe a teensy little piece of a white wall, which was my lover's cottage. The only connection between her and this patio are these mementos."

"In what way do you feel close to this woman?"

"We loved each other physically. It was an erotic experience, and that is a contrast to the Addams family. I have a warm glow, an afterglow from making love with her. I feel a sharp contrast between this feeling and the one before, of wanting to run. My muscles are relaxed. I feel a sense of well-being, and a sense of spirit."

"Is it related to the wings?" I implicitly interpret.

"I can feel it in my whole body, that sense of spirit. It feels transcendent. And yes, when I look at the wings it is particularly intensive."

"What happens to you when you look at the wings?"

"I feel like I can fly. Like the woman and I flew together."

"Where do you feel that in your body?"

"I have a sense of lightness. My breathing is easier. It's a feeling of the bliss of lovemaking. I had a sense of cherishing the wings. They were gifts from my beloved, so they have a very symbolic sense to me. Whether they are feathers or very thin tissue paper, they have that delicacy to them."

"The wings of love," a man comments softly.

"Yes," the dreamer agrees gratefully, apparently feeling thoroughly understood. For a short moment, we float.

Then we seem to sink. The shift of emotional ground is

felt the way a sudden change of temperature will send bathers inside for warm clothing. We wait.

"I just have a sense of great sadness," he begins. "I've always felt that my partner and I have the best relationship I have ever seen and that makes me sad. You just could not imagine a healthier, better, or easier relationship, which is not to say there wasn't trouble at times." The rhapsodic description of his relationship is verified by his intense sadness about the imminent loss. "The donkey right now seems to be walking in my direction," he suddenly says, spontaneously returning to the dream.

"What are its eyes like?" I inquire immediately, hoping this spontaneous self-presentation of the donkey will reveal the identity of the beast.

"I have a sense they are soft," he replies, squinting his closed eyes. "Even though it's got my shopping bag I don't have a sense of animosity towards it."

"Do you smell the donkey?" I ask, knowing that scents may reveal powerful emotional undercurrents.

"Yes. It is that warm, heavy animal smell, very much alive. The smell feels very alive, very organic."

"How does that lively, organic smell feel?"

"Effervescent and stubborn. I feel very good when I'm inside that smell." His spine straightens with vitality. "For the past five minutes I've had the image that the donkey is very close, so I can reach out and touch him."

"Do you?" I ask, slightly alarmed. I'm afraid the ego might move out of the reality of the dream, into the world of make-believe where Disney donkeys frolic as pets.

"I'd like to, but . . ." He hesitates.

"Is this your donkey?" I want to know, to establish his actual relationship with the beast.

"No, I don't have any relationship with this animal other

than being here." His tone of voice indicates a certain distance between him and the donkey. Glad I asked.

I return to the actual dreamscape. "How do you feel about the donkey holding this bag?"

"It is almost as if the donkey says, 'Well, are you going to take this or not? I'm standing here holding this bag.' "

"Can you smell the donkey again?" I ask, returning for a whiff of dream reality.

"Yes. This time there's a bittersweet quality to it. It's obviously not the same smell, but it reminds me of the smell of my partner. It's reassuring. There is a quality of the essential to it. It is that connection to life."

"A very stubborn connection to life. It doesn't give up," I suggest, holding up for all to see the donkey metaphor that has now firmly established itself.

"For me, that's part of the difficulty with my relationship with AIDS—that I, from the outside, get to the point that it's so difficult to bear other people's illness. I wish that they would just pass. I don't know how that will be for my partner"—he quickly expiates his death wish with a charm —"although we have had an absolutely blessed relationship and it has been absolutely charmed and I have a sense that dying will unfold with the grace that the rest of our relationship has. But I have seen other people with AIDS who have lingered. It's very painful to be around. The life force stays and stays and stays. When I think of my situation, it's very difficult to live in this context. There is such a disparity between his life energy and mine. I care about him so much that I hold back."

We all try to digest this love in conflict with itself.

"Do the wings offer anything to him or to you?" asks a woman.

"It's not so much what they offer to me, it's what they

represent. It's like the smell of the donkey. It's that same connection to life."

"Mementos of a cherished life," I metaphorize.

"Yeah, that's part of it," he agrees.

"Suddenly the donkey gets nauseous." I unexpectedly twist back to the plot.

"From having chewed on the rope." He cuts to the chase. "And I have this vague sense that I knew it was going to happen. My dream-self knew. 'Well, he has the bag and he is going to chew on it and then he will vomit.' I had a sense of what was coming. Then he spews out this very weird, almost glowing, very dense and gelatinous material. It's not like Jell-O. It's very formed. It's not quite rubbery. It has a luminous, glowing quality to it."

He spits out his sentences in staccato. I stick with the plot line for a moment longer, not quite sure where to enter the wild again, how to get back to the wilderness surrounding the narrow path of plot.

"Does the donkey feel relieved once it's out?" someone inquires.

"I would just have to make that up. I don't know."

"Time-out," I exclaim, and turn to the group. "See, here we're going too quickly. You can't feel at that speed. I don't want the dreamer to start making up things. I want him to stay with what is actually present. So we have to back up to the feelings of the dreamer before we can empathize with the donkey and feel what the donkey experiences." I return to the dreamer.

"When you say you know that the donkey will vomit after masticating on the handle, because you know there are chemicals in there the donkey can't digest, do you feel vindictive towards the donkey?"

"Exactly!"

"What does that feel like?"

"Smug, satisfaction. A righteous kind of quality to it."

"Does it have cruelty in it?"

"A little, maybe. It's like, 'Okay, go ahead, you have learned to do those kinds of things. Fine. You are going to get your due.' I have some sense that's the reason I don't try to chase after him. He is prancing around with *my* bag. With the bag my lover intended for me."

"Because you know he is going to get his due?" I remark with sadistic pleasure.

"Yep," he concurs.

"Do you know this feeling, this slightly vindictive feeling? It feels kind of shady, this satisfaction that he is going to get his due." I am treading gingerly in this sinister part of the woods.

"The association I have is not as strong as the feeling in the dream . . . but my partner doesn't have a sense of his limitations and puts himself in situations where he spends too much energy. I know he is going to overextend himself. But he cannot see that. And then he gets sick and deteriorates, and I pay the price."

"He bites off more than he can chew," a group member mumbles, as if to herself.

"He prances around while you have a sense that he is overextending himself," remarks another.

"Yes. And there is that sense of, 'Well, you got what was coming to you.' There is that vague sense when he is sick of, 'Well, I was right, I told you so,' because it doesn't do any good. He bears the illness with incredible grace." He pauses. He obviously adores his beloved. "But one of his weaknesses, which is one of my strengths, is that I have a better sense of how to shepherd his energies than he does."

His words seem to drift away in distraction. I need to know what's happening. "What do you feel at this moment?"

"I was just going back to the donkey. Trying to get into the donkey prancing around. *Liveliness* is too strong a word. It's almost as though he's showing off. 'Look at me with the heavy bag, ha, ha. . . .' There's a quality of playfulness, a little teasing. It's almost as if this is the natural behavior of a donkey. He does it because of being the creature that he is."

"Can you feel what that creatureliness is like?"

"It is being true to self."

"Can you feel his donkeyness?"

"Yeah."

"What does it feel like, that donkeyness?" I keep increasing the pressure. We are moving into the essence of this beast, and I want to condense the donkey sense of life to its highest possible potency.

"Like he wants to bray."

"And he likes to eat the bag."

"Uh-huh."

"Does he like the taste of the bag?"

"I have a sense that he wants what's in it, and that they are not his wings."

"He wants the wings, but he can't get them?"

"Yes."

"And instead it makes him nauseous. What does the nausea feel like?" I notice I'm gradually increasing the speed, as if to launch deeply into a visceral sensation.

"I don't want to say forbidden fruit, but this thing is not for his stomach. It is not donkey food. He can hold it in no longer and he vomits it out like a projectile. It comes out with a force, and it causes a stink that is pretty awful."

We feel revolted. "How do you first feel when you smell this?" I ask.

"It's pretty awful. It makes me dizzy."

"How does your body feel?"

"Sort of dizzy. It doesn't last very long."

He calms down. The first whiff of the utterly nauseating has passed. "The donkey seems to have stopped prancing," I remark, to note the calm.

"Right. He's got a fairly centered stance now. It's the little girl that swoops in so quickly. All the motion is in her now." Attention shifts to this new entrant.

"What about the little girl?"

"This weird sense of the macabre comes sweeping in. She goes after the biggest chunk—and I have a sense that she wants it for some macabre experiment. There is a lot of motion at this point. Things speed up really fast. She picks up the chunk and then I'm aware of the weird boy running around."

Another shift from relative calm to instant chaos makes me feel we're closing in on the center of an emotional storm.

"Can you get into that sense of the macabre that wants to make something out of the vomit?"

"It's not easy, because it's repugnant. It's unnatural. It goes against nature."

"What does that unnatural sense feel like in your body?"

"A lot of tension. It trembles all through me."

"It has a macabre unnaturalness to it," I note.

"I feel ninety percent repulsion, and this teeny, tiny bit of corrupt power. It's about controlling the forces of life, controlling the forces of the universe for this macabre experiment. It corrupts everything. That's the driving energy." That teeny, tiny ten percent feels like a description of the little girl.

At first the *fascination with the corrupt* is hidden behind the repulsion toward disintegration. Then it peeks around this revulsion to demonstrate the powerful attractiveness of its revolting face.

"Can you feel the corruption that wants to control the forces of the universe?" I ask, to get closer to the little girl's desire for experimentation with decay.

"Like claws gripping up and down my back and neck. It feels very contorting!" We can feel the discomfort rapidly becoming unbearable. The emotion has to erupt. It can no longer be contained.

"Can you feel the contortions in your body?" I give one last push, sadistically making him truly feel this repulsive force of corruption.

A gargling, contorted sound struggles from his throat. His body jerks with held-in eruption.

"Just let it come." I encourage the pain to surface.

He breathes loudly, as if he could vomit at any moment now. "It's hard to stay with," he groans, pleading with me to stop torturing him.

I muster all my capacity for cruelty in order to continue. Stopping at this point, however compassionate it might seem, would abort the process that could release the inaccessible, bottled-up emotion. Faint sadomasochistic echoes from a homosexual black-leather torture chamber reverberate, as I ask him with intimate cruelty to let it come. I notice this, and continue. "Can you go back again to the feeling of the macabre experiment," I insist, "of being involved in a macabre experiment? Just feel it." The pressure is now unbearable. He is twisting with the pain. "Just stay

with it. Can you say what it is like to be part of the macabre experiment?"

"It's torture!" he rasps. "It's like being twisted by
claws."

"And it's feeling you want to anesthetize." I inject the
final scene of the dream, where he sedates the hyperactive,
macabre children.

"I just want to be part of it!" he exclaims. "It is such
incredible energy. If it could just flow . . . it would be
easier. If the energy could flow through, it would be easier, but it's all bottled up."

"Where is it stuck?"

"In my throat. It clutches around my upper torso. I have
a sense of pressure, not just there but in my entire being."

"Just feel once more what it is like to be part of the
macabre experiment." I have to keep pushing. "Just feel it.
Just let it come through, just let it come."

The progression toward the breaking of the bottle in
this final movement of the work is jerky—almost reaching
crescendo and then receding again—like the halted progress of the strange, morbid vehicle of the macabre family,
like the dry heaves before actual vomiting. Motions and
impulses build up this way in dreams: the jerky motion of
the golf cart becomes the spasms of the vomiting donkey,
finally to become, at this moment under the pressure of
dreamwork, the agonizing labor that may give birth to a
remedy. Dreamwork has intensified tendencies in the
dream until they have become fullblown and irresistible.
Now, suddenly, he breaks out in an agonizing scream that
lasts for what seems to be an eternity.

He hyperventilates, then screams again. "It's like electric
shocks, like electric shocks!" We have reached the point

where the all-corrupting presence of death has the intensity of an execution.

After a long while, his breathing slows down.

When I ask him half a year after the work what he remembers from it, he tells me: "It was like the breaking of an egg, this experience. Before it I could not emote freely, but since then I weep about twice a month. Not like I used to cry before, but really weeping. That is a very freeing feeling. Before, I couldn't feel the horror and it froze me. That kept me under constant pressure."

The alchemists were right: at the heart of poison lies remedy. By pushing our way through to the core of the macabre execution that is AIDS, the egg broke open into new life. Like the refrigerator dreamer facing the essence of ice, this dreamer of the macabre has essentialized horror and a fascination with the corrupting power of death, until it turned into pure vitality. This follows a law the ancient Greeks had already discovered. They called it *enantiodromia*. It posits that any force, when reaching its full measure, will turn into its opposite. Independently, the ancient Chinese had called this the law of yin and yang.

Looking back over the work, some regularities come to mind: the sense of the macabre, essential to the work, arises first in the guise of Morticia. With her we can imagine skeletons dancing on the grave, the *danse macabre* from the days of the medieval plague. It is not surprising, then, that her daughter performs the macabre experiment. Without her experimental eagerness in the dream, the dreamwork could not have been done. It takes an almost cruel pleasure in the macabre, a morbid curiosity, to deal with this kind of gruesome material. And, short of dealing with it, the putrid, festering source of pain remains bottled up, feeding on itself, becoming a parasite, draining energy from its host. Common sense wants us to think positively, to suggest it is not all that bad, to present coping strategies. Though these may give temporary relief to the immediate emotional symptoms, in the long run they may be detrimental to the soul—and the body, as is demonstrated by this dreamer's constant indigestion. But the macabre eye sees that it is not just bad—it is much *worse!* Reality is terrifying to the point of being unbearable. It takes a compassionate eye of ruthless clarity for the awful reality of life as it is lived in the realm between living and dying, to allow the process of pressurizing the poison in the bottle until it transforms into remedy.

Sometimes we are rewarded, and after the poison is digested, the spirit is set free.

In dream practica I teach practical skills. We may use this moment of respite after a fateful meeting with the macabre and the power of corruption to reflect upon some techniques used in dreamwork. Let's look at *practical dreamwork technology.*

Imagine yourself in a pleasant place, where you can look out at an attractive landscape while you listen to me wearing my teacher's hat. (One of the last dreams of my Australia cycle says that life is a story of many different hats.) It will give you a chance to daydream and have your thoughts trail off. . . .

Like the alchemists of old, who, unlike modern chemists, worked on matter they did not rationally understand, a dreamworker deals with the unknown through her work on dream material. Alchemists worked on their material with imagination and dedication, in order to facilitate a transformation of the matter at hand. A dreamworker acts upon dream material in a comparable fashion.

Alchemists called *acting upon* material *operatio.* Alchemical operations included building a fire, beginning with the right materials, putting them in the proper vessels, and heating and mixing these materials in hermetic vessels so they could transform into new alloys.

In dreamwork, *amplification* is such an operation. Amplification makes an image reverberate with *similar* images and stories from our collective consciousness: our fairy tales, myths, anthropological reports, TV programs, movies, literature, cartoons, poetry, gossip, art, news, and religion. This reverberation amplifies, as it were, the signal contained within the image so that it becomes audible to the conscious mind. Amplification pumps significance into an image until it spontaneously bursts into awareness.

My descriptions of the traveler Mercury in connection with the Leiden Academy dream are amplifications that led me to the insight that this dream was an initiation, changing me from a youthful nostalgic into a solitary man overwhelmed by the certainty that we move around in many realities at once.

In the dream about the insecure President in his White House, with the nonpterodactyls rising up from the pit behind, we can amplify the element "white" with fairy stories of innocence, political propaganda about white supremacy, the whitening (albedo) in alchemy that refers to the dawn of a new awareness after a dark night of the soul, or the heroic white knight in shining armor in the romantic popular imagination (for example, the cowboy with the white hat, the good cop, Indiana Jones). All these images are alive with significance. They surround us like radio waves, constantly feeding our imagination whether we're "tuned in" or not. By focusing these tales of our collective dreaming on a "personal" dream image, the image begins to hum with resonance: suddenly I notice the insecurity of the presiding "superior" white mind, heady with scientific convictions, about to lose its innocence in the dawning of a new, archaic day.

Interpretation is another operation in the alchemical sense of *operatio*. With interpretation, *timing is everything*. Usually it is best to think of an interpretation not as right or wrong, but as well- or ill-timed. Interpretation usually takes place in later phases of dreamwork. *Premature interpretation* is a defense of the city-walled, habitual self against the incomprehensibility of the dreaming wilderness. Since interpretation leads us from dreaming toward meaning, it tends to make us lose track of dreaming reality itself.

Interpretation usually has a drying, astringent effect, like alum on a bloody wound—and in fact it can often be employed to stop a flood of emotional bleeding. One example of a well-timed use of this drying effect comes from a practicum: after the dreamer had spent a long time in desperate confusion, a woman whispered to her that this confusion might be connected to a childhood situation the dreamer had revealed earlier. The interpretation was delivered very lightly. (Almost imperceptible lightness is the hallmark of a subtle interpretation, one that bypasses the walls of the city of self—sometimes a simple pun, without emphasis, does the trick.) Suddenly the dreamer realized how her critical mother—both as an historical (exterior) and as an introjected (interior) presence—had always made her feel incompetent. She had stumbled upon the source of her present state of confusion. The interpretive connection made by the dreamworker instantly transformed the dreamer's foggy state of confusion into one of realization—into the clarity of a dry day when you can see far into the distance.

If the interpretation had been offered too early, the dreamer would not have been close enough to the wound in her soul, would not have been sufficiently drenched with the pain it continually caused her, for the interpretation to have its transforming effect. The pain of utter confusion had to be fully experienced for the resulting, concentrated state of clarity to emerge. And the more concentrated a realization is, the stronger its *therapeutic* effect will be on the psychological system. This therapeutic effect is an important product of dreamwork—modern Western dreamwork was born, after all, in the consulting rooms of physicians. A premature interpretation, on the other hand, would probably have been the result of a *dreamworker's* inability to stand this dreamer's miserable confusion, her spinning atmosphere of gray haze and dull sounds. Each experience needs time to fully ripen. It is the task and challenge of a dream group or a dreamworker— or an observing aspect of self—to hold the dreamer still in the uncomfortable position of waiting for feelings to mature, while at the same time providing a firm enough sense of safety that the dreamer will be able to stand the discomfort.

Structure analysis studies the logic with which an image is constructed in the same way an engineer looks at the construction of a bridge or an artist looks at composition. In the White House dream, the archaic pit of ghost-winged nonpterodactyls is the backdrop for a meeting of the Secretaries of the white mentality. It is a foreground-background composition: white in the foreground, dark in the background. The nonpterodactyls can be seen from the point of view of the white Cabinet, while the white men can be viewed from the perspective of the archaic spirit that arises. White in contrast with black/red, foreground vs. background: any analysis of the image that does not take these compositional aspects into account overlooks an inherent logic of the image.

Common *structural elements* of dreams are *contrast, paradox,* and sudden *shifts* or *changes.* In the White House dream there is a stark contrast between the birds and the Cabinet, the White House and the pit, presidential authority and insecurity. A shift or change takes place at the moment when, suddenly, the pit appears. Each of these structural elements may be used as a pivot around which to hinge dreamwork. The work may focus on the inner conflict within the president's mind, using the transiting technique. We may feel ourselves into the birds, then into the Cabinet, and experience the difference. We may sense the symbolic import of the White House and contrast it to the pit feeling. Or we may focus our attention on the suddenness of the presence of the birds, the sense of archaic eruption.

Structure analysis is particularly important for dreamwork in respect to *pacing.* I understand pacing to be the allotment of dreamwork time to various elements of the dream. The shorter the time available for dreamwork, the higher the pace of the work has to be. The motto of alchemy is, *Hurry slowly!* It is the slowness of the work that leads us down to the depths. A higher pace does not mean racing through the dream images at great speed. That would just be a kind of channel surfing—exercising our skill with the remote, at a safe distance from emotional impact. A high pace is based on the selection of a *few* essential elements of the dream. When the pacing is high, the dreamwork has to be ordered within the available time span according to the structural *hinges* in the dream. On the other hand, dreamwork is virtually endless. The longest I have ever worked on a single dream (in a group) was for eight hours, having exhausted only ourselves but not the dream. So, in fact, all dreamwork suffers time limitations. The dreamworker paces the work in such a way that there will be enough time left when points of highest resistance are reached. Long dreams usually require high pacing.

In order to facilitate adequate pacing, the dreamworker, after the second telling of the dream, decides on a *strategy* concerning the movement through the dreaming: where to begin, which points to touch, and where to end up. This strategy is then *dropped* at the first available opportunity; the strategizing serves primarily to make dreamworkers aware of the amount of material in relation to the length of the dream and the available time.

The hinges I employ most frequently for pacing are contrast and paradox. Contradictory feelings are valuable for the expansion of our ability to contain conflicting psychological material without bursting. A *conscious experience of paradox* stretches the soul. Such a paradox can be found, for example, by contrasting the feelings embodied by the boldness of the idea of a White House at the center of Western power and the experience of being a bottomless pit affording access to a world that is fundamentally different from that of modernity. I can sense the power of the White House in my tight right arm and fist—the ambient mood of the White House is an environment surrounding me from all sides—while the left side of my body simultaneously senses the background radiation of the open pit, making me feel like a bag, open to infinity, a cringe of fear in my heart. By trying to feel both parts of my body at the same time, the body built right and the anxious, aching left, I observe a central divide running like a crevasse along the core of my body. My White House walk is strident, my left side goes barefoot. My right side feels heroic, like the white marble statues populating monuments in Western capitals; my left feels like a child floating down a river through a dark jungle. The difference creates tension. I try to hold this tension for a while, even after it has become unbearable. My right sees this as soul calisthenics —training the muscles of soul the way an exercise machine trains the pectoral muscles, widening the chest. My left-side self feels that elements of myself are being essentialized. For a moment a more essential self exists, partaking in a world of conflict without repressing anything that lies on either side of the divide. I am right, left . . . and the divide. I am paradox. I am truly myself.

Working with *contrast* is impressionistic in nature. It consists of feeling the wide range of experiences a dream has to offer, like the rich variety of colors one sees in an impressionist painting—each color itself, each color giving the one it contrasts with a different hue, each contributing to a total effect. I feel the insecure Clinton, the soaring birds, the decisive members of the Cabinet, the sense of the table between them, the darkness of the pit. I feel my way through each of these elements to its visceral presence. It is similar to the work on paradox described above; however, in working with contrast, I keep mixing the shades of color without choosing two that are particularly opposed.

This impressionist work often gets short shrift because working with paradox is emotionally quite spectacular. An insight into how working on paradox can be seductive

came in one of my dreams while in Australia, as the voice
of new people:

> **Some new persons at the dream practicum are discussing
> the method. They are saying that it is just as interesting to
> see what makes things change. My Tokyo dream group co-
> leader laughs and says, "We go from the assumption that it
> is possible to feel what the other character is feeling. But
> that is just an assumption, because maybe we cannot." I
> listen very carefully and say, "That is a good idea, to see
> what makes things change," because I myself am dissatisfied
> that we always end up in this paradox. It is always the same
> —and we agree to try to follow how things change. I say this
> is a good idea because the Jungian problem is that you al-
> ways end up with the paradox. It becomes boring.**

Obviously, in this dream I, in my teacher-of-dreamwork
hat, do not want to face up to the challenge as to whether
the identification technique I have developed—transiting
—is really possible after all. Yet I do accept the notion
that a routine movement toward paradox eventually leads
to a feeling of "So what else is new?" A careful observation
of the experience of change is what really seems to matter.

As mentioned in previous chapters, observing *physical
sensations and mood changes* while listening makes us receptive
to possible symbiotic communication. As I described to
Ilyatjari through the example of the balloon dream, these
self-observed changes in atmosphere may be seen as indications of resistances. (Frequently, in dreamwork groups
and practica, it occurs that those who sit very close to the
dreamer have the strongest physical and emotional experiences to the dreamwork. It seems that *proximity* enhances
symbiotic communication.)

Any form of mental distraction while listening, most prominently boredom, might also point to *resistances*. Resistance is signaled in the—conscious or unconscious—experience of being repelled. In dreamwork, *wherever we feel ourselves pushed away, there we start swimming against the current*. To enhance my awareness of resistances, I therefore take notice of any moment when I lose contact with the dream. It may happen that I can't listen anymore because I get tired, begin to drift off, or have other thoughts come into my mind; I may get bored, want to leave the room, even want to never have anything to do with the dreamer again, and so on. Such distractions may point to places where the material repels me, and this repulsion may indicate a radiation produced by a protective wall around a painful wound. Dreamwork assumes—recalling Mercury's rule over both poison and remedy—that the remedy for pain is made from the wounds that cause it. This movement against the current of psychological resistance also calls to mind the alchemists, who considered their work as *contra naturam*, a movement against the natural order of being. They did not, to coin a phrase, go with the flow.

The interaction between waking consciousness and the dreaming imagination Jung called *active imagination*. It was one of the techniques most frequently used by the alchemists in their work on the depths of their material. It is a dialogue between the reality of dreaming and the probing conscious mind.

Unlike lucid dreaming—as in the Leiden Academy dream where I know I am dreaming—active imagination takes place while being awake; it occurs on the waking side of liminal consciousness. The experience of the reality of the dreaming environment is considerably less absolute in the case of active imagination than it is with lucidity. However, active imagination can be achieved at any waking moment and, with some training, more or less at will.

I differentiate between two forms of active imagination: *bound* active imagination and *free* active imagination.

Bound active imagination is used in the service of dream recall. It tries to move as closely as possible along the contours of the dream *as it is recalled.* Our dreamwork on the scene with the woman in the bar showing the photograph to the man provides an example of this. Similarly, the experiment in Chapter Three, leading toward identification with another dream person, or transiting, is a form of bound active imagination.

Free active imagination is what Jung calls "dreaming the dream onwards." Free active imagination starts with an authentic image (I usually prefer to begin with a dream image, so I won't start out with an ego invention) and lets the authentic action unfold from there—while the waking self remains constantly aware of the reality of the images it observes. Jung said that if, during active imagination, you see a lion on the Bahnhofstrasse (the main shopping street in Zurich) and you don't respond with heightened alertness or a sense of fear, you are not in active imagination, because it is not real to you. (For this reason, expecting such a lion to speak to you always seems odd to me. A lion is a lion is a lion, wherever you meet him, be it in the jungle of Africa or on the Bahnhofstrasse of your dreams. If the lion wants to speak, that's his business. But if you *make* him speak, you're probably inventing things.) Another hallmark of true active imagination, be it free or bound, is the occurrence of entirely and sincerely unexpected events. If the imagination unrolls in a predictable fashion, you're probably doing some screenwriting.

To ensure that we don't move too far from the dreaming, we regularly move from free imagination back to dream recall. "Let's go back to the dream" is a sentence often heard in dreamwork—especially if there is a feeling that the dreamer is beginning to invent things.

One of the ways of noticing whether an image is authentic or invented is by way of *gauging depth*. In the balloon dream I described to Ilyatjari, I gave an example of gauging depth.

I imagine dreamwork as scuba diving. As you get deeper down inside the dreaming, the pressure increases. This is experienced as increased concentration and diminishing observation of events taking place outside of the dreamwork. While dreamworking in a city, the police sirens that whine constantly through the evening begin to fade away. The discomfort of the chair you sit in vanishes. Time opens up into another dimension. When you come up from some deep dreamwork, it is often surprising how much (or how little) time has passed: depth time is often different from surface time.

While the atmosphere gets denser, the experience of the image becomes more visceral. The flimsy sense of the image decreases. At the same time, the sense that you are looking *at* an image transforms into a felt experience of being *inside* the image. The image gradually surrounds you from all sides, just as physical reality does.

Here you have a direct experience of Jung's most important discovery, of what he called the *reality of the soul*. You realize, with Jung, that soul is not in you, but that you are in soul. Soul is an environment surrounding you. On the level of dreaming reality, soul is landscape. Jung and Ilyatjari would agree on this. In her depth, soul is ambient.

When you find yourself inside the world of the image,

you have acquired depth in the dreamwork. At this point images are more stable. They don't flitter around like random daydreams, but keep their form for a certain period of time. When this begins to happen you usually find yourself in a state of deep concentration, with a sharp sense of focus. The surrounding image has become very dense, and the experience of this reality you are in is often accompanied by physical sensations, bodily reactions to a palpable atmosphere.

It is important to be aware of the fluctuation of depth during dreamwork because it is a good indicator of resistances. When resistances increase we are often pushed up to the surface. Often, in dream groups where people work with their eyes closed, you notice participants opening their eyes at the same time: they have been pushed up to the surface simultaneously by a source of resistance. (To dive into depth again—when, and if, we want to—it is useful to employ detailed dream recall. This leads us into bound active imagination and back into the deep.)

Because of this feature of dreamwork, whereby the work takes place on various levels of depth, questions we ask the dreamer should correspond to the level of depth on which the work is presently occurring. Working on the balloon dream, it would not be useful to ask the dreamer about her mental associations concerning policemen at a moment when she is viscerally experiencing the sense of being in a straitjacket. The straitjacket sensation is taking place on a deep level—as demonstrated by the accompanying physical sensations in the chests of both dreamer and dreamworker—and a question about her day-to-day experiences with police would lead the dreamer back up to the surface, out of her body and into her mind. Such a question I call a *context* question. I usually ask for context before I actually start working on the dream, before we enter into the material and move to the point where we are surrounded by the image. In this way I can insert these responses to my context questions into the dreamwork, without losing depth.

Often, at a point when an image is being acutely experienced, and the dream atmosphere has thoroughly penetrated the dreamer, I will ask, "Does this remind you of anything? Was there any time in your life when you had a similar experience?" This is a request for *associations*, and it superficially looks similar to, but actually is quite different from, a request for context information. It makes a major difference whether such a request is proposed on the surface, as context questions are, or at a level of depth, where the whole person is engaged with the actual reality of the dream. The request for associations leads to an export of the moods and sensations present in the dreamwork to the biography of the dreamer, creating connections between what is felt in the dream and memories of the past—and an import of the sensations connected to these memories back to the dreamwork. The dreamer who was led from her disoriented fog to an acute sense of clarity as a result of an interpretation by a dreamworker in a practicum remembered how her critical mother had always made her feel incompetent. Associations flooded to the surface around the mother and the self-hatred she had caused in the dreamer. Associations often lead to a *flashback* into memories that have lived with the dreamer as physical sensations, frozen in a state of physical memory. A pain in the chest felt when facing an unknown man in a dream of a dark parking lot suddenly brings back that night, long ago, with that horrible baby-sitter. Tears flow out of the pain in the restricted chest, as if the symptom were melting into pure emotion, and the dreamer breathes freely, as though she had held her breath ever since that fateful night long ago.

There are two other forms of queries I differentiate between: *clarification* and *intensification* questions. A clarification question leads to a further description of the dream, to get a clearer sense of the image we are dealing with. These questions are usually asked at the beginning of the dreamwork process.

When clarification questions are asked for too long a period of time, the feeling of being stuck at the surface of the image becomes uncomfortable. At this point it is important to shift toward intensification. Intensification questions serve to hold the dreamer in an image so that the pressure may build, and the image is given time to deeply penetrate the dreamer's awareness. Such questions are often repetitive, and the art in the work lies in asking the same question in many different ways so that each question comes at the same event from a slightly different angle. ("How is the person moving? What is the motion of the spine? Is there a bounce in the step? What happens to the neck? Does the speed of the motion remain the same? What is the rhythm of the movement?")

As the finale of my little technique-teaching riff, my use of the word *flashback* brings us to the movies. I love movies.

Since dreams are usually very visual, it is useful to refer to cinematographic tools and procedures like *lenses, pans, slow motion, freeze-frame,* and *fast-forward.*

We may begin to look at our dream surroundings by means of a pan with a wide-angle lens, to get our bearings, then slowly zoom in on an element that needs more focus.

By intensifying the focus, more pressure is put on the detail and it begins to reveal itself.

A woman gets bitten by a dog and her wound festers.

First we focus on the entire attack with the use of a wide-angle optic. We experience the atmosphere of the entire event. Then we zoom in on the wound in her thigh. It festers. She feels she has been entered by disease. Using a macro lens, we have the wound take up the entire field of consciousness. Suddenly dread is everywhere. Now we create a freeze-frame of this experience by prolonged focus. This dread of violation turns into a sense of having been soiled. She remembers a rape and a loss of innocence. Then she feels very sober amid the mayhem. During the freeze-frame emotions transform.

A man goes downstairs to a room he has never been in before.

With the use of slow motion we focus on the move of the foot from the top stair to the one below. The man suddenly realizes that if he takes this step, things will never be the same. In slow motion we experience the hesitations, hopes, and fears in the decision to explore the unknown.

We all have rooms downstairs we have never visited. Their unknown nature both frightens and fascinates us.

CHAPTER 8

Tracking
Your Own Dreaming

DREAMS ARE PART OF DREAMING, AND DREAMING IS A STREAM THAT constantly creates worlds. There are many dreams, coming one after the next. Some of the most recent dream research shows that dreaming takes place not only during REM (rapid eye movement) sleep (sections of sleep during which the eyes move rapidly behind closed eyelids), as had previously been thought—two hours of dreaming per eight-hour night—but occurs as well during other states of sleep (previously considered dreamless).

Professor Marino Bosinelli, an internationally respected dream researcher from the sleep laboratory at the University of Bologna, Italy, wrote to me:

"Since the non-REM period includes stages 1, 2, 3, 4, the following data concern both the sleep onset (descending stages 1 and 2) and the Slow-Wave-Sleep (stages 3 and 4). As far as the sleep onset is concerned, the percentage of dream recall ranges from 65% to 70%."* "Following

---

*M. Bosinelli, P. Cicogna, and S. Molinari, "The Tonic-phasic Model and the Feeling of Self-participation in Different Stages of Sleep," *Italian Journal*

Slow-Wave-Sleep awakenings, the percentage of dream recall ranges from 64% to 77%."*

If I understand his data correctly, this must mean that out of an eight-hour sleep, some six hours are spent dreaming (two hours of REM plus four of the six hours of non-REM sleep)—a grand total of twenty years of life spent in a state of dreaming during an eighty-year lifespan.

Therefore, it is essential to look at dreams not only individually but from a serial perspective as well. From this viewpoint, we look at dreams as existing in a continuing state of context, in relation with each other. Like the spaghetti of dreaming tracks (aka song lines) crisscrossing Aboriginal Australia, continuously intersecting and veering away from each other, along which in the dreamtime the ancestors cavorted and dreamed up this world, the dreamworld tells tales that follow along interconnected lines. Individual dreams are like individual sites one visits along the song lines of one's dreaming. To see the images of my thinking paralleled by a people we had not met in fifty thousand years, who had become separated from us when the Ice Age ended, was moving, to say the least.

Dream moments connect to others along thematic roads and highways throughout the dreaming. This I call the *infrastructure* of dreaming.

In his 1935 Eranos lecture, C. G. Jung was the first dream researcher ever to work on a chronological report of a group of dreams *as a series* in order to understand

---

of *Psychology*, 1:35–65 (1974). Also M. Bosinelli, "Recent Research Trends in Sleep-onset Mentation," in S. Ellman and J. Antrobus (eds.), *The Mind in Sleep*, 2nd ed., New York: Wiley, 1991, pp. 137–142.

*C. Cavallero, P. Cicogna, V. Natale, M. Occhionero, and A. Zito, "Slow-Wave Sleep Dreaming," *Sleep*, 15(6): 562–566 (1992). Also M. Bosinelli, "Mind and Consciousness During Sleep." Symposium on "The Function of Sleep," *Behavioral Brain Research, 1995.*

unconscious processes. This lecture appeared later in his book *Psychology and Alchemy*, one of his central treatises on the lost art and its intimate relations to dreaming. The dreams he used were of one of the great scientific geniuses of our century, Nobel prize-winning physicist Wolfgang Pauli (nicknamed by his fellow scientists "the Conscience of Science"), who had done dreamwork with one of Jung's close colleagues. Thus, the work on dream series came, so to speak, from the night of science.

The most difficult part of dreamwork is working your own dreams. Without outside help from a dream group or an individual, it is hard to prevent yourself from being swayed off course by resistances.

The best method, then, for initially finding your way through the dreamworld is to begin with a dream series. A dream series, by the time we draw up reports of remembered dream events, consists of a chronologically ordered set of stale dreams—but in this case the stale nature of older dreams actually proves to be an advantage. It is as though we have been removed light-years from the events and look back at them over vast oceans of forgetfulness, and this makes it possible to see the distant constellations, clusters of similar forms that appear throughout the various dream narratives. In this way we discover tracks through the dreamworlds we have lived in. The distant starscape becomes a landscape we can map.

As an illustration of how one works with a dream series, I have chosen seven weeks of my own dreaming, starting with the day I arrived in Australia and continuing up to three weeks after my return home. The last dream of this series was followed by a spontaneous hiatus in my dream recall of several months. My journey to Australia was part of a change in the seasons of my life; this dream series elucidates this changing of my worlds. Dream series during pregnant periods of one's existence—when new life incubates—are well suited for an in-depth scrutiny of their infrastructure, which shapes a kind of fiber-optic network in dream space.

I blush to think of all the revelations about my own nature I am now unwittingly presenting. Others can always see more in our dreams than we ourselves can. I would not feel free to publicly divulge such amounts of intimate emotional material concerning one of my patients.

I am strengthened by the fact that these dreams are not particularly different from the over twenty thousand dreams of others I have been privileged to observe and enter into over the past twenty-three years, in many different places around the globe. Yet, I would have had no need for the previous sentence to bolster my self-image, if I weren't extremely embarrassed at this very moment. I appeal to you for clemency.

Method

Let me emphasize from the beginning, and I can't say it strongly enough: *work on your own dream series is about the process of doing it, not about the outcome.* The product you end up with is irrelevant, compared to the change you go through when you seriously set yourself to do this work.

These fifty-three entries, made over a period of seven weeks, give a detailed report of dream events during a contained time span surrounding a vital life experience:

my journey to the upside-down center of another world, where I discovered the effects of my father's passing.

In the appendix at the end of the book I have included fifty-one of the entries in my dream log of fifty-three dreams. Fifty-three is an almost unmanageable amount of dreams to work with. I suggest you start with less than twenty.

I would also suggest that, in reading through this serial dreamwork illustration, you first read the rest of the book and only then turn to the appendix with the actual dream log entries. With such a large number of dreams, there is so much material that the nature and function of each step might actually become blurred if you right away try to trace my steps through the actual dreaming. Better to follow through the example steps first, then see the dream log material from which my examples arise—and then, perhaps, return to the examples in order to get a complete understanding of each step.

Step 1: Making a Dream Log Foldout

Type up or print out your dreams in small print, single spaced, on eight- by eleven-inch sheets of paper. As you can see from my dream material, I write up my dreams in a fairly concise manner. The text is just enough to make me able to reaccess the dreams while they are still fresh.

Spread these pages out on the floor, facedown, each connecting on the vertical side with the next, containing in chronological order all printed dream log entries you want to process. From this make an accordion foldout— using transparent tape on the back—by folding the scroll at the tape. The foldout contains the remains of a wilderness of dreaming. From a distance it looks like a horizontal scroll with vertical columns.

Step 2: Making a Map and Infrastructure

Take a pencil and a ruler and begin to connect all images that strike you as similar: the resulting infrastructure creates a map. To accomplish this, read through the entire text slowly, familiarizing yourself with the images. In the second and later readings go for connections. Some people find it helpful to use different colored pencils to indicate various thematic interconnections. (I'm a black pencil type myself. My infrastructures look quite messy even though I do use a ruler to guide my pencil from one point to another—a long ruler, that is.)

This is very painstaking work. Expect resistances. At first the material may seem impenetrable, daunting, and entirely unmanageable. It is patently too much to handle. It feels like you've undertaken a ridiculous task anyway. You may feel foolish to honor the nonsensical with so much attention. These are all clues that you must continue. They are eruptions of your fear of the unknown, thus indicating you are penetrating into not-knowing.

An example of making an infrastructure: A woman friend my age discusses divorce while seated at a long table (1). In the next dream (2), I find a long table leading up to a wedding. I draw a line of connection between the two "long tables," and note that divorce and wedding are the opposing ends of marriage. Long tables return at the wedding of my best friends (39). Now I'm on a roll, and note that references to weddings are all through the material. *Marriage* must be a central theme.

Step 3: Identifying Clusters

After you have spent time tracing an infrastructure through the material, begin to look for clusters: thematic connections that weave through the material by way of the dreaming tracks you've identified in building your infrastructure. I have distributed my material over thirteen clusters. These clusters serve as initial containers of the material, bins for storage.

Example: Cluster A: Marriage, Depression, and Loneliness   A woman friend my age discusses divorce while seated at a long table (1). I find a long table leading up to a wedding (2). Long tables at the wedding of my best friends (39). The nineteenth-century couple waltzes while I ask her to marry me (35). Long tables at a conference (17). I feel ineffective at a conference (3). I feel disappointed because people haven't come to listen to my lecture at the conference (17). I feel ineffective in general, because I don't write anything, whereas others are loudly applauded (3). My wife is gray and old (1). I look exhausted (3); I am bored and lonely (1). I've run out of gas (32).

Step 4: Musing

After making an infrastructure and identifying clusters you let yourself muse over the life of one of the clusters (repeating this and the following steps with each cluster).

Example: Life in the doldrums; running out of steam. If weddings are rites of renewal, then I'm in dire need of one. The married status quo feels pale and gray, boring and unsatisfying. I cannot find my own ideas. I feel impotent and very uncreative, while others are profusely productive. There is trouble in marriage. It has dried up. At the same time new weddings take place. Is this a time of death and renewal in marriage, or just of death? Will it be just impotence, or an unconscious regression into the roots of being in order to find new potential? There is talk of divorce, *and* dressed in full nineteenth-century romance, I ask her to marry me. What's it going to be? I'm worried.

Step 5: Reminiscence

Take some of the dream images that strike your fancy and begin to reminisce about the past. I chose dream (35), which reads in part:

> **We are on a space mission, as in *2001: A Space Odyssey*. We're being brought to the earliest intermediate station, on the moon. There, one of the women takes me and shows me around. It is a dark place. It is probably night. She says, "Oh, come, I'll show you the place where it all started." She takes me by the hand and runs me over to a cave. We enter the cave. . . . The transformation happens immediately. We are waltzing. And we're clearly in the nineteenth century. We've traveled back in time. She has late-nineteenth-century clothes and I wear tails. The room is large. Everybody around is waltzing. I say in German, "I want to marry you." And she answers in German, "Yes, I also want to marry you. . . ."**

My parents met at dancing lessons in Cologne, Germany, when he was seventeen and she fifteen. He was Dutch, she German. She had long dark braids, which he would drape carefully over her chest as they won competitions in the Viennese waltz. This is what I've been told about the genesis of my parents' relationship, which ended with his death sixty-two years later. The dream waltz reminds me of these events resulting in my existence. The experience is strange and incestuous by association. Oedipus, your father is dead: mother is free.

Step 6: Writing Along with the Cluster's Chronological Format

Use one descriptive paragraph for each element of the cluster, in chronological order.

Example: Cluster B: Students   A student of mine is very upset about the changes in the way I work (16). We're sitting on a veranda talking together. We're all young students (20). We break through the wall and everything is in motion again; cf. one of the early Australian governors' theories positing that the Academy is in constant revolution, constant motion (22). There are students who come to my aid when I'm accused of sexual malpractice (25). I'm in a large room with many pictures around, a real student room from my student days (26). Talking about Pitjantjatjara at a Jungian conference; experts are very upset that I speak about this. It should be kept in the area of experts. A young man, a serious student of these matters, says: "We've done all these studies and now . . . you're holding it up by walking behind" [literal translation of Dutch idiom meaning "not being up to date"] (27). Students break into the library to get beer; earthquake follows (32). New students at a dream practicum are discussing my method and want to see what makes things change (34). The young man I'm attracted to resembles a gentlemanly fellow student I looked up to in my student days. He asks how big my . . . is (I can't decipher the word in my dream log [sic!]) (48).

The sight of students conjures up the days when the mind was free to play; days of library and beer! Days that shook me like an earthquake, by way of physical illness, out of familiar constraints into the open sea, breaking down the stultifying walls of my background. From a student of law I became a student of psychoanalysis, not by choice but by necessity.

We sit on the verandah and talk sophomorically about topics of interest. Everything is urgent and nothing matters. Yet, some certainties matter. They are not to shift. If they do, there is hell to pay. They shift. A world collapses. Am I in a rerun of the sea changes that happened in my student days?

My student protests against the changes; a conservative voice is heard. A young man who has made studies in areas where my new ideas are considered half-baked protests that I will damage the field. They'll see me for the fool I truly am. I quiver.

All I know about Governor Macquarie of New South Wales is that a university is named after him near where I taught my Sydney dream practicum. I have no idea what theories he stands for, let alone his position on the idea that learning has to always remain flexible, in a constant state of revolution. My governor of the otherworld-of-old declares that change is never-ending, and turmoil the natural state of thought. And he asserts that within this constant turmoil higher learning takes place.

A great classic of the Orient is *The Book of Changes*. My dreamwork students, new to the craft, wonder about how change slithers its way through dreams. What existed one moment in all truth, vanishes and is replaced by a world equally real and totally different. In the dreamworld the excess of existence makes space for itself. There is too much life spouting up from the deep to be satisfied with one single reality. The soaps keep on coming. The beginner's mind in my dreamwork wants to observe how the book of changes is written in our dreams. Teaching of a higher order values impermanence. The Genius of Perpetual Change is the one whose song line I—like Nganyinytja and her Ngintaka tracks—steward: I keep it fresh by sharing my dreams of the songs and dances of change with the culture at large, whereby I myself am changed. In my culture, the god of changes is called Mercury.

When Robbie is in trouble, when he's falsely accused of sexual misconduct, students come to his aid. I feel supported by this past, by these student days of youth, innocence, and faith in others, while the present-day nightmare of sexual allegations hangs over all therapists like a sword of Damocles. This student environment—my real student room from olden days—is full of images that create wonder at a time when thoughts are fresh. Yet sex is on my mind while authorities accuse me. Am I up against a voice of sexual morality, and is that related to my feelings of impotence?

Among other manifestations, the desire for change appears sexually. I'm frightened of the way I am attracted to the early twenties of life in the guise of this delicious and noble young man. The fear of my gay impulses coincides with my student friend's question after the size of my I-know-not-what. Gay desires and competition mix together: Let's see who's bigger. These realizations would have frightened me no end during my actual student days!

Step 7: Rewrite the Material Obtained by Step 6 in Various Genres

Write a letter to yourself with a story that contains the cluster's elements. On the basis of these elements, ask yourself questions. Or some clusters are better served with a travelogue, others with a poem—or writing of any genre that fits the mood.

Example: Cluster B: Students   Genre: Translation of a secretly taped conversation among old Dutch cronies reminiscing about their student days, after several rounds of beer.

Crony 1:   I remember how we used to sit on the verandah shooting the breeze. We were free then. You could think anything you wanted. Everything was urgent and nothing mattered. When you were in trouble, falsely accused, other students would come to your aid. You'd support each other. Sex was free, then, remember?

C2:   I used to love my room. I had it full of pictures, full of images that create freshness and wonder.

C1:   You need another beer. Get this guy another beer.

C3:   I used to get very upset when people changed the way they worked. When you suddenly couldn't trust that what you wrote down in the beginning of the year was still true by the end.

C4:   You're so conservative! That was just the fun of it. Everything always changes. That's what you have to learn in college, how to be flexible, because everything changes all the time.

C5:   You sound like that old governor from down under. He said that the Academy should be in a constant state of revolution. If the mind can't keep on changing, you're dead! At least that's what they think in that other world down there. Remember the days of rebellion, when we occupied university buildings and knew the world was ours for the taking? I loved the six-

	ties. Today is just work, work, work! Or being out of work.
C3:	[asks C5] Didn't I see you run out of the bathroom? Why were you running?
C2:	I know! I heard that kid, that student, ask him how big his . . . was. He must have gotten scared. Look, he's blushing. I didn't know that about you!
C6:	[Reconstructed from garbled speech] Earthquake. Everything shook up. Broke away from family. Everything to pieces.
C1:	You've had enough. Don't let him have any more, he still has to drive.

When you come upon a section that reminds you of a story you've once heard, weave it into your text. This is what I described before as "amplification." It will bring significance to the surface because the dream images will bounce off a surface of similarity. You can also weave in a contrasting story. In Cluster L, called The Long Trek Home, I wove in a contrasting story about Plato's cave, and a similar story, Proteus' prophesy.

When you have finished working with any step, let it rest. Take time to reflect on your emotional responses to the work so far.

When you've set it aside for a while, come back to it. This time, try condensing narratives: take your musings about the clusters and highlight those elements that matter most to you. Switch clusters around, seeing whether a different order or different juxtapositons of the material give rise to new insights.

● ● ●

Show your work to someone else. In my case I showed it to my wife. It produced fireworks!

Continue to read everything over as slowly and as often as you like—or can stomach. This is your dreaming; these are your dreaming tracks; this is your landscape.

Finally, let it rest. You have done all the work necessary; now give it time to work on you.

The serial dreamwork presented here was the fruit of over two months of labor and digestion. I'd work for half an hour here, an hour there; then suddenly it would grab me and I'd work for a few hours straight. At one point my schedule sent me away on a trip. When I returned, I saw all kinds of things that hadn't struck me before. After such a period of unconscious digestion—such as the time I was away on my travels—go back to your accordion foldout and study the lines of connection you have drawn. You will notice new connections, and old connections will make new sense.

Following are the other clusters and the pieces I wrote based on the elements of each cluster.

Cluster C: Sweet Women　　Home alone I am bored and watch an erotic flick (1). I'm being stimulated by a young woman, a generation younger than I. We have to *stop* (4). A young woman at the Springhouse *stop* sells me sweets after I leave the sick old man (15). I sit with an attractive young woman. I tell her I'm married. We're disappointed we have to *stop* (16). Young women undress but are *finished* before I reach orgasm (29). In my childhood home the love of my adolescence calls me to her room; she's as beautiful as when she was twenty (38).

Letter to myself

Dear Robbie,

Your marriage feels stale and you want to step out. But every time you try you're stopped. You long for the freshness of youth and you feel caught inside marriage like a spirit in a bottle. The exits are blocked. Will marriage transform, like material in the hermetically sealed bottle of the alchemists—where rot is integral to the process—or is this to be decay without redemption? You have to stay put in this compost heap of matrimony, yet the sweet love of youth calls loud and clear with the voice of a passion that never pales. What will you do with middle age?

Cluster D: Mysterious Communication   Cable TV will be all over the world (5). An evil stepmother-type woman and her daughter, both dressed in bright red, are frightening ghosts: a frightening women's mystery (5). A ghost stands by a bright red door leading to another world (6). The prehistoric birds coming out of the pit have bright red wings (11). A communication system has been developed that will give universal access (11). In the new world, communication is everywhere, by way of elegantly feminine units (11). I have to lecture about the Eleusinian mysteries, the women's mysteries (17).

Dear Robbie,

From below the earth, a place you don't know, prehistoric birds with bright red wings fly up while a ghostly woman in bright red frightens you. You want to get away from her because you are so scared. But you're forced to get in touch with the frightening mystery of woman. You thought you knew what feminine sensibility was all about. Well, you got it wrong. You spent entire days with women, hearing their deepest secrets, yet still you know nothing. Why does woman frighten you? Is that why marriage feels so stale? The mystery of woman has to be learned anew. What you thought you knew about woman has now become a hindrance. A new communication with her is foretold. Apparently, with your father's death not only your manhood changed! Your femininity (whatever that is) did as well. What does this new feminine communication look like? Does it have to do with symbiotic communication? This new connectedness may remedy your feeling of impotence, the drained sense of being alone, of being out of touch, of having run out of gas.

Cluster E: Mother   The queen is at the wedding (2). My "stepmother" becomes a frightening ghost (5). The mother below brings up her children with beating and fear; the children vomit; she's much too rough (10). My mother berates my vivacious uncle. She feels she has to carry all responsibility (13). I bump into a woman looking and acting like a depressed patient I used to see in therapy, who dragged me down like no other and was always in love and enraged with me. In the end she changes into my mother behaving bitchy and slighted, putting me down, accusing me of vanity, of wanting a Nobel prize, while in truth it was her vanity (18). A woman's mother dies of a heart attack (33). At the wedding I embarrass myself in front of the mother of the groom (39). Mammie, my mother, finds it entirely correct that Annie's friend is so angry with me; it is deserved (47). Pappie, my father, seems to be getting over his illness and Mammie wants to start traveling again. She wants to go to Paris (50).

Letter to My First Analyst

Dear Aniela Jaffé,

Do you remember that when you took me on I paid you very little, because I was a poor student, or so it seemed? When it appeared that I was less poor than expected, you raised my next-to-nothing fee a tiny bit. Do you remember how you suddenly turned in my mind into the dark mother who rejects me? Well, these dreams have happened to me and they are about her.

In them she seems overburdened, depressed, deflating, righteous, and longing to get a vacation. Furthermore, a mother's ghost frightens me, a marriage-mother puts me to shame, and a mother dies, like my father, from a heart attack.

Is this my Depression Mother, the deadly one, the one from below who tortures her offspring until they are sick and vomit? The rejecting one who was not invited to the christening of Sleeping Beauty; the one who, with her daughters, picks on Cinderella. You knew how this dark mother frightened me and how I wished her away. This time she's shown her origin: I bump into a mental hospital patient of mine—hospitalized for years because of a psychotic depression—who gradually evolves into someone whose irritation is like that of my actual mother. However, the essence of the person I bump into remains that of my extremely depressed patient. My children called her "the Psychobitch from Hell," because of her constant desperate calls from the hospital for help and her suicidal messages. Her clamor for my attention drained me to the bone, yet I could not disengage from her. She was scornful of me, punishing me for each distraction from her. She pushed the limits to the utmost, so that I constantly rejected her which made her even more outraged. This is the female I'm afraid of, the devouring one of draining depression and depletion. The one with nothing to give, just to take. The Evil Witch from every fairy tale. Yet, my actual mother had been a warmhearted, supportive, good woman whom I truly love, which you never doubted. And so my analysis truly began when you became the devouring, rejecting one. When even your gentle self became threatening. That is when we found my depression lurking in the deep which had haunted my mother's family for generations, ready to suck out each last drop of energy. Well, I'm there again. And it's my wife Deanne this time who gets the brunt of it.

The most scornful sentence mother speaks berates my desire for a Nobel prize. I make it clear to her that this had been her wish, which shuts her up, because it's true. She needs me for recognition, she is my vanity. This desire for recognition I was complaining about in my notes when I went to Australia this year is fueled by this frightening ghost-mother's vanity, as well as by my father who needs love and attention and who is, like me, the little brother of a big brother.

I just wanted you to know.

Cluster F: Sickness, Fear, and Dying   Pappie had been very ill, he had almost died, but didn't (13). A friend of Annie's is not in the least bit interested in me (9). The friend of Annie's is still angry with me because I had deserted Annie when she was dying (47). After birthing the mucous insects, I have to go to the hospital and share a room with an uncle who died (9). A mother living below brings up her children with beating and fear; they vomit (10). Faced with a choice between the old and the new, I join the old and become terribly nauseous (14). Old Ethan is very ill; I desert him (15). I see a man in a wheelchair; a romantic woman dances me out the door so I never get to meet him (15). I am afraid of the room behind this room. The black dorsal fin of a land shark follows my wife through the outback at a lower level of the dreaming trail, cutting just above the surface of the red earth as though it were an ocean. Very scary (16). I remember being at the funeral of a colleague of mine called John, like my brother. He had died of AIDS (actually, this John's *brother* had died of AIDS). I took half of his ashes to the outback (19). There is black earth, black sand, and I have a pain in my chest (21). There is an earthquake and everything collapses (32). A woman dies of a heart attack (33). The stairs collapse and fall down (36). In the dusty barn everything will have very little time (37). The fantastic building disappears, entirely decayed, out of this world (39). Pappie had been very ill but was getting well again. I remember that I have been at his funeral and that the father in my arms is both dead and present (50).

Confession

When Pappie, my father, had his heart attack I was in Moscow, staying at the studio of a painter friend. I was told that it had not been serious although he was in intensive care, and that he had insisted I should not interrupt my trip to Berlin where I was to teach next. Work to him was almost sacred. I did not get to talk to him personally. Telephone communications between Moscow and Rotterdam were cumbersome at the time. I got up from the bed where I had received the news and tried to convince myself that he was not dying, stretching the calming words of my family to their utmost—until I realized the next day that I had to go home. I called off all engagements so I could be at my father's bedside the day after the next. My wavering made me late by eight hours. Like with old Ethan who is ill, I wanted to shake off old age, illness, and death from my youth-bound life.

When I grew up, Annie was my best friend. She understood me and she was the only one who talked to me about Auschwitz and after. She broke the ominous silence of the imageless nightmare my elders thought they could protect me from by not talking about it. That's probably when I first found out that moods exist as ambience, without ever having to be expressed. I was in love with her cultured strength and the melodious timbre of her voice. She was ten years older than my parents. In her eighties she fell and had to move. I knew the uprooting was the beginning of the end. For the first time she showed me her new apartment. I had scheduled a second meeting later that night and saw her for barely an hour. Death won't happen. "I will see her again," I told myself. I did not. I feel ashamed. Death is so frightening! Denial is immediate.

In one dream Pappie had almost died but didn't really. . . . Pappie hasn't died yet. Dying takes forever; it's now three years past his physical death and he still has to go through a dying in my soul, which clings to an "almost but not really." I realize that with his death my love for him has not died. This is a first step to let myself know that he is truly dead. At the end of the dream series I *know* that he is dead. In the beginning I embrace a father who is alive; at the end I embrace a father who is vibrant, yet dead. Why is dying so long and life so short? There is a barn full of dust. Ashes to ashes, dust to dust. It is said that all that comes from there has only a short span of time. Between dust and dust, between ashes and ashes, a life is a moment. I remember the last conversation I had with my father. "It has all gone by so fast," he repeated. I could see that in his tired old body the spirit of youth was still wondering what had happened.

Death lurks right below the surface, where a shark makes his way underground and a dorsal fin cuts through the earth. He's after my wife. He wants her dead. No doubt I have a death wish toward the one who seems to drain me of all life. This time it's Deanne. Also, the cutting threat of death follows us in our tracks, wherever we go, inescapably.

I can't return to the old world. The world that made sense when my father was alive, died with him. I get sick trying to hold on to the old. I need to gain flexibility, to allow for change. I'm petrified.

The earth is black and I feel a pain in my chest. Will I die the way my father did? I'm next in line.

Cluster G: Brother Love My brother, John, had preceded me to the wedding in the "Inner Court" with the queen. The younger brother of the *other* bride comes up to say a word: a struggle between him and the bride (2). My father's older and only brother, the bon vivant, is fighting with my mother (13). Ethan, the older man who looks like my father's brother, is very ill when I abandon him in favor of the girl who sells me sweets (15). The woman, whose annoyance sounds exactly like my mother's, is on her way to the coming of age (bar mitzvah) of the only significant *other* boy from early childhood through adolescence called Robbie. She chides me for wanting a Nobel prize (18). I'm told I have the *other* part of the ashes of my colleague John, whose brother died of AIDS. His ashes were split at the funeral. I'm told that when I went to the bush, the Center, I took these ashes with me (19). In my brother John's room the delicious women arouse me by undressing. The question is: "What will you become?" (29). One of the brothers is to commit a murder. One of the *other* brothers, young Ethan, will kill the prime minister (30). I'm visiting the brother of the older woman (31). Jerry, aware that I am in a double world, is my brotherly guide through Australian bachelor nightlife (41). I ask a man to get in touch with Jerry for me. He says he doesn't know Jerry (42). In the toilet I am strongly sexually attracted to the male lover of Jerry's brother; he asks how big my . . . is (48). The *other* Robbie takes me to his home on the park named after the queen who had presided over the weddings in the Inner Court (49). My brother John drives the car, with me in the back holding my father in my arms. I know that John is at the same time not John (50).

Just Telling It as It Is

My brother came first to the Inner Court of the queen. He was in my mother's womb before me. He was the young male I grew up behind, always a few sizes smaller than him. He was the Big Bosnak, to my Little Bosnak. How big is your . . . ? Competition!

My father was a younger brother, too, and shared with me a longing to be seen, developed into a passion for recognition. ("To think that you believed that you would get the Nobel prize!")

When I came to the center the first thing I wrote in my log was: "This unquenchable thirst for recognition is stifling my creativity. It makes me worried about how I'm being received, if people like me. It makes me search for honor, not substance. I share this with Pappie, a sucker for honor as well. Recognition swells my head but does not satisfy."

The younger brother of the *unknown* bride—I had come to attend the wedding of the bride I knew—struggles with his sister. The unknown younger brother wants attention. He wants to be heard. To no longer be unknown? He struggles for attention in the eyes of the queen. How different from my conscious perception that *I* was Mother's favorite!

A roaming brother is on the prowl, a desire to kill on his mind, to murder everyone who dares to constrain him. Is it his wife? Kill her! Is it the epitome of authority, the leader of the country? Death to him! He wants to be free of care. To be a bon vivant; to live, as did my uncle in his youth, a carnival with a woman on each knee. The young one wants to abandon responsibility and everything that is old and decrepit. But at the same time, I've gone to the center of things—where I deal with brothers dying of AIDS all around. I feel responsible. I bring Ilyatjari, the eagle father, my AIDS dreaming. I feel I have to deal with all the death around the brother world. There is a battle between the longing for the freedom of youth and the necessity to take on the father, to be responsible. What will I become in a world where *I* am the father? I'm moving into my dead father's spot, the new authority, the next to die.

Brother love turns sexual. I'm attracted to the young lover of my friend's brother. What will my desire for change do to my sexual imagination; does this brother lust frighten me? I run out of the bathroom where I meet with this gay attraction!

But that is not the only love among men that emerges. In the back of a car I hold my father in my arms knowing full well he is dead; yet the love between the two of us is stronger than it has ever been. I experience a moment in which it does not matter that he is dead, since the other world is real. The veil between life and death lifts momentarily. His death has entered me.

The driver of the car that drives the love between me and my father is my brother John. The driver is not my brother John. Simultaneously! The biographical image I have of my brother John is at the same time an entirely different autonomous entity, driving me through the world of father love, of love among men. Two worlds as radically different as life and death exist at the same time and it matters not a bit.

Cluster H: Two Worlds   A *double* wedding takes place at a place called the Inner Court (2). There are two worlds (6)(7), a twilight zone (7). Two spirits in love want to pass through from the otherworld to this one. We are in a place that doesn't exist, the alien replies after entering this world (7). There is an ordinary room and a frightening room behind it (16). The lovers whirl from one room into another, where he finds his voice (17). Death is like going to another room (33). We're running into a wall and break through (22). A man breaks into the unknown, into another world of constant change (23). My Japanese co-therapist says: We go from the assumption that it is possible to feel what the other character is feeling. But that is just an assumption because maybe we cannot (34). We are exploring an unknown planet (24). There is an outer world and a world inside a can (40). I know that I am in two worlds at the same time (41). When two spirits inhabit the same space they each become less real (43). The detective from *Roger Rabbit*, experienced in the double world of humans and cartoons, helps the naive Robbie (45). I ask a woman who is both an actress and not an actress to marry me (35). The driver of the car is both my brother as well as not my brother.

Earth to Robbie!

Your life has run into a wall. In order to get unstuck there is an urgent need to break through to another reality, to set up communication between this world and another. It seems your world has been one-sided, which explains your lack of voice, of ideas. You've not been open to voices from the other side. Creative impulses got stuck because your view of life had you separated from the reality of death. Your fear of death jammed your channels. You see a room behind this room; it frightens you. It is said that death is like going to another room.

You break through the wall and get to the other world, a world of constant change. Your experience of death must have altered to allow for this breakthrough. Life meets death, this-worldliness meets other-worldliness, Europe meets the red center, Western consciousness meets wilderness, man meets woman. Two worlds exist at the same time—life has become relative. Now that two worlds of such fundamental difference have become connected, woman has been restored to her mystery—has once again become a truly unknown world that has to be explored. How will that affect your thought and, more importantly, your marriage? Also, who are these dreamworld beings now that the world has become double? When you see your brother in a dream you know that he consists both of the experience you have of him and of a dream being presenting himself as your brother. You propose marriage to this doubleness, asking a woman who you know to be simultaneously real *and* an actress—mere appearance. Doubleness will be with you forevermore.

p.s.: Transmission report, recently received, of research conducted in another world (41): While I was in the reality of another world, in a post office to communicate with the world back home, I did an experiment to investigate the difference between this other world and the world back home. I closed my eyes and recalled this post office the moment before my eyes closed. Then I imagined it. Imagining it was very different from actually being there, because when I opened my eyes, everything around me in this post office was real. I felt it, I knew it, and I could touch it. It was completely and totally real, while, when I imagined it with my eyes closed, it was wispy and not nearly as real. Conclusion: The difference between recall and actuality is the same in the dreamworld as it is in the physical world.

Cluster I: Hats I have two good hats; to my horror a little child-painter smears paint all over them; they are ruined (31). Pappie is wearing his white cap (50). This is about different hats (51).

Essay for elementary school called "Hats" to be read in front of the class in a small, high voice.

Hats are important to me. My grandfather was born in the 1860s. He was a hat maker.

I have two hats. My one hat is a Stetson, like the cowboys wear. My other hat is an Akubra. An Akubra is an Australian hat.

We went to visit this little three-year-old kid who put paint all over them. Now my hats are ruined. In my hat is my head. All my thoughts fly away without a hat. Now both my American and my Australian heads are blown away.

My father loves his white cap. It makes him look sporty. He loves his cap clean. My father has white hair. My father is old. My father is dead. Are ghosts white?

This was a story about hats. There are many hats. One for every mood, one for each head I'm in.

Cluster J: Transformations A frightening mystery. Suddenly the "stepmother" is gone. A message is left on the answering machine. She returns with her daughter my age, yet each twenty years younger and looking very pasty and frightening; they're ghosts (5). First it looks like mucus, coming out of my penis, then like worms, then fresh sweet shrimp (like amaebi sashimi), then an insect with wings, long legs, and antennae with the slimy consistency of a snail covered in gelatin (9). We have to study how things change (34). Suddenly everything changes. It is a tremendous shock, though I know it is happening (35). At first the building is new and beautiful; then it quickly becomes ancient and disappears (39). A game at the wedding had a person go through transformations all the time. It had to do with the notion that everything was meaningful to a ridiculous degree (39). At first we come to a room where women are baking; their skin looks like a soufflé of egg white; one of the women is suddenly under water and her head shrinks (41). In the other world I see the picture on my driver's license actually disappear as I show it to the man behind the counter (41).

To a Stranger on the Train

There once was an older woman in my life who felt like a stepmother to me, a stepmother of the Cinderella kind. I can't say more. And indeed, she had a daughter my age. That was the first time reality suddenly changed on me. It scared me to death when she suddenly became a ghost. She felt like a Great Annihilating Mother, eating me raw. I told you that this devouring mother had been the subject of much of my first analysis. Very depressing. Life would be hummin' along and suddenly everything would change. The world would grow dark and frightening from one moment to the next. Most often it would come just before a creative spurt. Therefore it is not surprising that I spout new life after meeting with her, slimy globs of new mutation.

Then there is this matter of my identity. The strangest thing happened: as I was holding my ID in my hands the photograph vanished. I actually saw my identity vanish before my very eyes. It took place in the other world. What do you think it means that my identity is erased? I'm confronted with a dissolution of identity in this time of transition. It must relate to this dream I told you in which my sex organ tears as I give birth to disgusting primordial globs of unformed life. I am a birthing male. What is happening to my masculine identity? Eventually the transmuting life form appears with the sensitive antennae of a slug, feeling the slightest change in the environment, pulling in when threatened and expanding with curiosity. A winged sensorium, soft like the life inside a shell, is en masse exposed to the world. Maybe now that my likeness has dissolved, it proved to be a shell, and behind the shell a new sensitivity is born. Is this part of feminine communication, or the sensitive softness of new masculinity; What do you think? Don't answer! Sometimes I worry if with all this new softness I will still rise, stand, and deliver like a man. . . .

It is change itself that matters, new students of my way of dreamwork tell me. Indeed, what dreamwork has done for me is that it made me adjust to changes in the environment faster than before—important when every workday you live in several radically different worlds for pay. It keeps you flexible. It also helps jet lag. When change is what matters—truly a mercurial perspective—then there is great need for sensitive antennae to get a quick feel for the next reality.

In this critical time of change, my major life changes come into view: I'm in the lunar cave where dreams are made. The world suddenly changes from nineteenth-century Europe to twentieth-century American Midwest or Texas. Each immigrant can appreciate the shock to the system. I moved from Europe to the United States in late 1977. The change from tails to dirty T-shirts and suspenders has tremendous impact, yet I am encouraged to observe the coexistence of my European and my American life. I'm receiving lessons in versatility.

Someone's head is made of airy soufflé. It is held under water and shrinks. Head-shrinker, shrink thyself. . . . Am I boring you? Hey, are you sleeping? Did you hear anything I said?

Cluster K: Wings   Repulsive gelatinous winged insects issue from my torn genitals (9). Archaic reptile birds spread out their ghost-red wings from the dark pit next to the White House (11). Nauseated by my decision to stick to the old, I awake to see a gigantic eagle, with a wingspan crossing the sky, fly overhead (14).

POEM

What first seems mucus,
through dreadful parthenogenesis,
becomes a living spirit of its own,
ready to fly.
May seeking sweet seduction
by the young
be a desire for anesthesia
so as not to feel the pain
of giving birth?

Reptilian birds, long gone from Nature,
emerge from where
the center of the white world stands.
The sky is filled with ancient sounds

of wings within,
forgotten by the surface of the earth.
Forever, it had seemed.

But archaic wingspan has returned,
propelled by glowing red of ghost.

The wings grow fast,
embrace the sky.
The eagle seeks the galaxy
where Ancestors dwell.

Then a flash of lightning.
It begins to drizzle.
I get up to cover
our belongings.

The Sky spirit and
the flash of Nature
are mixed together
in marriage.

The meeting of nature and image
strikes sparks of thunder.
It is no longer obvious
what happens outside
and what within.
The worlds are a continuum.

Cluster L: The Long Trek Home [American Heritage Dictionary—"trek: . . . a slow and arduous journey . . . from Dutch *trekken,* **to travel."]**   Boat wants to leave (11). I see a book in the bookstore about my life outdoors. The color pictures of me look very rugged. I'm very trim (17). The return: going back over an enormous distance (19). I'm going into the outback and it is known that the most important experiences are in the dark and unknown (23). In the mountains: the morning program is over and a woman tried to convince me to go trekking. I'm on the trek; a slow trek is much more introspective; young Ethan the assassin is going down the mountain fast (30). We're going to a village nearby to see the older woman's brother; I'm told to disinvite curiosity (31). Earthquake; I have to go home; the whole village is after me; my motorbike won't start (32). The whole Australian village is after us to trap the woman who has returned to visit her childhood home (33). A woman is dying; we wish her a good trip, a good journey (33). We are on a space mission to an intermediate station on the moon before going into deep space (35). Someone takes us to a mountain. There is a very fast race; two people fly in free-fall very deep down; the stairs back up collapse (36). My alter-ego finds an ancient map. He travels through many adventures in different periods and is able to hold on to the map. Finally he sees at the source of the river a building called "blueprint of the world." A transformation game is played that has to do with the notion that everything is meaningful to a ridiculous degree (39).

A Travelogue

I can hear the foghorn of the boat. The journey is to start.
    I haven't produced very much.
    In this uncreative mood I find my publisher's catalog. It is a thick booklet and has many color photographs of me in it, outdoors. At first it looks as if they have published

many of my lectures. I am happy that so much of mine is in print. Maybe I'm more productive than I think. Then I see that the book is called *The Life Outdoors*. The photographs are very rugged. I look trim and healthy. I don't have a double chin. The photographs are in color. This production by Robert Bosnak, the author, I hadn't known about. It takes place in the wild outdoors. The wilderness stimulates my health and ruggedness. It gives me color.

I have traveled to a faraway world where machines carry consciousness. Any fan of science fiction, as I am, will understand that I've traveled into the future where human consciousness has given birth through silicone. In this distant mental world ideas now exist independently from us. The mind keeps on creating by itself. How far removed from where I find myself so uncreative! Obviously it is a long trek back to the present. I have to go back to my home in the past over vast distances. Mind reaches back for body. The disembodied thought of deep space has to come down to earth.

The return home, to the time of origin, goes by way of the outback, where all that is known is that the most important experiences take place in the dark and unknown. These travels take place in the deep unknown.

The morning program is over. Life's sun has gone past zenith and is returning to the night. I'm over the hill, as they say. Time to prepare for what is on the other side of morning. Yet I want to keep on skiing fast, to keep the speed of youth. But the bindings are old, no longer safe. A slow trek is the order of the After-Noon. Youthful skiers can manage the ice. Others free-fall into the deep. A fall of no return, since the staircase back up is rotten and drops. "Your own risk," I am told. "We'll paper it over."

We're now in a life at the bottom of the steep, down from the peaks of youth. I'm forty-five when I dream this.

Setting out on this afternoon trail, I first visit the brother of the old woman. I enter the home of the old couple. (I'm reminded of a saying on a restaurant wall that reads: "Forty is the old age of youth, fifty the youth of old age.") I have to enter the house of age. But curiosity has to be left behind. It is not invited. I had always thought that curiosity leads to knowledge. Yet curiosity may also prevent encounter. I remember sitting with my old uncle, incapacitated by paralyzing strokes that eventually killed him. I looked at him, curious as to what was going on inside his mind. He got very annoyed and exclaimed in an accusatory way, "Watching, watching!" I felt ashamed. What for me had been a curiosum, to him was his life. (He was the uncle in whose hospital room I ended up after birthing the slimy snails. Not curiosity, but shared suffering matters.) Curiosity may not just kill cats, it could prevent encounter. My student-of-other-cultures self should keep this in mind, as should the explorer of the world of dreams.

I come to a geometrical building, possibly octagonal. Some kind of library. I am standing outside. Suddenly there is an earthquake. The whole building turns and collapses. The library, the world of mind, is twisted to an unbearable degree. The mental construct collapses. The ivory tower of learning lies in rubble. All that is left is ignorance, and the desire to get back home. I try to go back on a motorbike. It won't start and I don't know how it works. A friend of my son's may know how to fix it, but I have no idea. The motor of youth is out of gas. I want to go back home! I'm being held responsible for the earthquake that has shattered everything in sight. The villagers are after me. This alien world is persecuting me. I want out.

After a long chase where we're persecuted by villagers, similar to the ones before, we come to the deathbed of an old woman. She is certain that dying is like going to another room. In the conviction of her faith she looks young and peaceful. We sing "Amazing Grace." The trek I'm on this afternoon is the journey of death, a movement to another room.

Etched in my soul from my first major death—that of my grandmother, a month away from her hundredth birthday—is the last moment we were together a few hours before she died. Suddenly glowing within the wrinkles was her spirit of youth. Her face shone. At that very moment we were young together, loving each other in springtime. We both felt this moment to our very core. Then we parted.

The space odyssey has reached the intermediate place between Earth and deep space: the moon. The moon, with her shining silk beauty, womanly menses, and dark brooding moods, reminded our ancestors of the cyclical change females are wont to experience. Her nocturnal ivory-mirror light populates the world with imagination. A fellow astronaut, a woman, leads me to the lunar cave where it all started, the womb of "it all." The cave becomes a ballroom in the nineteenth century where I dance with my beloved as I ask her to marry me. Then, suddenly we're in the American Midwest at a gas station. It is entirely real, yet all is in the lunar cave. In this cavern entire worlds change into each other in ongoing discontinuity. In the cave of lunar imagination worlds come into being constantly; new lives are lived all the time.

On page two of the first piece I ever wrote about psychology I retold the parable of the cave from Plato's *Republic*. The cave is by far the most famous image in Western philosophy. Let's give the floor to Socrates, father of our Western thought:

> Picture men dwelling in a sort of subterranean cavern with a long entrance open to the light on its entire width. Conceive them as having their legs and necks fettered from childhood, so that they remain in the same spot, able to look forward only, and prevented by the fetters from turning their heads. Picture further the light from a fire burning higher up and at a distance behind them, and between the fire and the prisoners and above them a road along which a low wall has been built, as the exhibitors of puppet shows have partitions before the men themselves, above which they show the puppets. . . . See also, then, men carrying past the wall implements of all kinds that rise above the wall, and human images and shapes of animals as well. . . .*

What these people in fetters, continues Socrates, would see, would be the shadows cast on the wall before them and the echo of the words spoken. But as they do not know better, they think these appearances are reality. One man is freed of his bonds and turns around. After a long struggle he ascends to the light of first the fire and later the sunlight. He is blinded and confused. Then he remembers his former dwelling in the cave and feels compassion for his fellowmen and returns to tell them of his experience.

The Collected Dialogues of Plato, Edith Hamilton and Huntington Cairns, eds., p. 747. *Republic*, Book VII, trans. Paul Shorey, Bollingen Series LXXI, Princeton, N.J.: Princeton University Press, 1973.

Would he not provoke laughter, and would it not be said that he had returned from his journey aloft with his eyes ruined and that it was not worthwhile even to attempt the ascent? And if it were possible to lay hands on and kill the man who tried to release them and lead them up, would they not kill him?*

Socrates foresees his future, self-murdered by the citizens of Athens for his philosophy.

I've called up the cave at the source of Western thinking because it *differs fundamentally* from the lunar cave I visited on my trek. (And possibly because, with all my odd notions about other worlds and symbiotic communication, I expect a similar welcome as the man who returned to the cave.)

Socrates' cave is very familiar to us today. We call it the movies. Plato, who relayed Socrates' words to us, describes a captive audience that has never been outside the theater, convinced that movies are absolute reality. In Socrates' cave, as in the movies, the images themselves are illusion; in my lunar cave they are entirely real. For Socrates, the only reality is seen in the sunlight outside the cave. "My" intermediate lunar cave honors the moon's inner musings, which are as real as can be. Socrates' idea rules the *solar* world and has informed Western consciousness ever since, having us rip away appearances to find reality. On the other hand there is the moon, enfolding the realities we encounter at night. Night is as real as day. At night, appearance is all there is. In the *lunar* cave what appears is real. In this moon cave I ask a woman who is simultaneously actress (appearance) and real, to marry me. To the

---

*Ibid., p. 749.

night there is not a hierarchy of realities, one being more real than another, but many realities exist simultaneously. To our dreaming existence appearance *is* reality.

I've returned home to Holland to be at the wedding of my best friends. I see the bride, my wife's best friend. She is upstairs. She's dressed beautifully, wearing a gown of old silk. She shines like the moon. I bow to her and she laughs. She is surrounded by all her bridesmaids. Then I find a map. A very ancient map. I am now someone else: a straw-blond fellow student with a classical Latin surname, whose father had been ambassador and had a home on a Greek island. An apt protagonist for an odyssey. I (becoming him) find the map. There is a drawing on it. The drawing has an X inside a square, with an onion-shaped dome on top. The drawing as a whole reminds me of an hourglass. With this scroll he treks through many adventures, living through every possible human experience. My alter ego has to get through many different lives.

In the end he comes back to the wedding with the scroll under his arm; he has been able to hold on to the scroll through all his trials and tribulations. But the wedding is over. The long tables are empty and the chairs lean against them. It's a feeling of after-the-great-party, which he has missed entirely. He goes over to the river and sits on the grass, dejected. Suddenly he sees a building to his left, at the source of the river. The building is exactly like the drawing he has carried with him through all the many lives of trial and adventure. Above the square base of the two-level building, right under the onion dome, it says: "This is the blueprint of the world." He looks at it and I stand next to him. He sees it and it is fantastic to behold. Then it instantly becomes very old. It disappears, entirely decayed, out of this world. It looks like the whole building is driving off; it goes away. The building had been made of wood; old wood. It was a geometrical form: a square box (the square, I am well aware, is a medieval symbol for *matter*) containing the X of the *unknown*, topped by the onion dome of the Russian *soul*. In the Russia I have encountered, West meets East, Orient meets Occident. The whole building looks, overall, like an hourglass, symbol for *time*. This "blueprint" at the source, this *original* design, shows the way the eternal unknown—in a meeting of cultures—is contained in matter, soul, and time. At first it had been new and very beautiful. Then it very quickly became old—because it all happened long, long ago—in a once-upon-a-time time, a dream time. I tell him: "I have enormous respect for you, that you held on to the image. Because you did that, the building has truly existed." For a brief moment *originality* existed in all its luster.

The permanence of change doesn't faze this blond fellow who travels the Greek isles. When a transformation game (called "the game of meaning") was played at the wedding he went through all kinds of changes. Once I saw him sit somewhere as a dressed-up animal, an elephant in clothes, looking like the Hindu god Ganesh, Overcomer of all Obstacles.

I would feel embarrassed about this adventure, which feels meaningful beyond belief—a kind of *conversion experience* in which the meaning of it all suddenly becomes apparent, like St. Paul's on the road to Damascus—if I had not known a tale from antiquity about another blond one, Menelaus, who tried to find his way back home from Troy among the isles of Greece. Since I'm on a long trek home myself, I might as well mirror my odyssey with the original one. A storm tossed Menelaus toward the island of Pharos. There the daughter of the Old Man of the Sea told him to ask her father, who had the gift of prophesy, for the way home. It was midday and Proteus, the Old Man of the Sea, slept among his flock, the seals. Menelaus seized him. Proteus began to shift shapes, from lion to serpent, panther, boar, running water, and leafy tree. But Menelaus held on to him, so finally Proteus had to prophesy: "Return to the river Egypt and bring the gods the sacrifice you owe them." After doing so, Menelaus returned home to his Helen after eight years lost at sea. Proteus' prophesy reminds me of Nganyinytja's words, "Maybe you have not properly fulfilled the rituals of burial. Maybe there is still something you should do for the dead."

Menelaus had left his home to reclaim the beautiful Helen he had lost. He left from an empty, barren home and returned to one of beauty. I also have to reclaim Helen for my home, which otherwise will remain dull and boring.

There is an essential shape within all the shifting life experiences. If you can *hold on firm to all appearances* and not let them escape from your grasp, you will eventually find your way back home, to the blueprint at the source of the river. Humans, too, have a *homing device* the way homing pigeons do. Ours has been diffused by layers of rational learning. To my surprise I find that the death of my father has sharpened this homing device now that I have to go entirely my own course. The world had been my father's domain, and even though I lived in faraway America, his encouragement had been the voice from home that helped me find direction. Now that the worldly voice from home is silenced, my own homing device surfaces. It gives me a sense of the essential within the manifold appearances, a sense of direction through the wilderness of dreaming. It keeps me connected to the source of my being.

According to the Protean myth, this "blueprint" speaks with the voice of truth, much like the escapee from the cave speaks truth after seeing the sunlight. It speaks of a single right course of action. There is only one truth. This *one* ultimate truth is real, just like the *many* intermediary lives in the quixotic lunar cave are as real as they present themselves to be. "One" is a dream different from "many." The One God and the Many Gods exist simultaneously, each a total cosmos. Both dreams—the lunar cave of many and the single blueprint of ultimate truth—follow each other in quick succession, both real like the double reality prefigured in the double wedding in the second dream in a place called the "Inner Court."

The revelation of the blueprint of "it all" surrounded the wedding of my best friends. A new point of orientation has entered marriage, a new way to befriend it. And what is marriage, if not home?

But has it come in time, or will I be too late, like when my father died? The wedding is over; the chairs lean against the long tables. The adventurer has missed the wedding. Have I missed the marriage? Will *this* Menelaus ever reach his Helen back home?

Cluster M: Going Public My Viennese psychiatrist friend has just realized that the publisher he has been looking for is in the building right across the street looking like a parking garage (8). Talking about Pitjantjatjara at a Jungian conference; experts are very upset that I speak about this. It should be kept in the area of experts. A young man says: "We've done all these studies and now you're holding it up by walking behind" [literal translation of Dutch idiom meaning "not being up-to-date"] (27). I'm distressed because I forgot my video camera while on the moon (35). Before I can tell my experiences with Aboriginal people, I have to let the can show (40). I'm in a temporary post office in the other world and have to send boxes of things back home (41). A teacher shows how things have to be done together with the Western mind; yet when it really gets started, the Westerner has to leave. We're waiting for the right moment; the spirit doctor is no longer [I believe "no longer" is accurate] or not yet [this may be wishful, upon awakening] in his strength (44).

A Year Has Passed

In the beginning was the desire to go public, but not knowing how. Yet all that needed to be done was to look across, to the other side.

Experts, those in the *know*, were angry that I talked about people from the other side—in their manifestations both in their Pitjantjatjara *and* as the dreaming populace. Only those who knew, not dilettantes like me, had this area for their own territory. A beginner should not yet speak. (At this point still, I hear my critics only with my inner ear of dreaming—after I go public all of my ears will hear them.)

First the experience—now (like a movie) in the can—had to be shown. I had to show what's in the can. I had to digest the material by revisualizing it, editing it. Only then can the material be made public. I had to wait.

The Western mind—the mind of experts in the field of science, strict Western logic—was needed to help the process gain momentum and contain it at the same time. We had to hold on to Western logic until it unraveled by itself in the face of the spirit doctor's world. Yet the spirit doctor, who waxes and wanes like the moon, was diminishing. I wished things were different, that the spirit were waxing. My impatience was felt in almost mistranscribing the dream experience. A whole cycle of waning and waxing had to take place until the spirit would once again be full. Until then I had to cooperate with Western sensibility. I recall Jung's resistance to his Chattanooga barber. Maybe the time had not yet been ripe for fresh kinks in his Western mind.

A year has passed. It is August 1994. I have returned to the heart of the red Center, at the great rock Uluru (aka Ayers Rock), to do a final rewrite of this book. Now, at last, the experience is in the can, ready to be projected into the world.

CHAPTER 9

My Old Man

AT THE END OF MY AUSTRALIAN DREAM CYCLE A DREAM APPEARS convincing me that now is the time to work on all the previous dreams. This book is a result of this conviction. The talk I am about to give in the following dream (52) is essentially the content of this book: Australia, symbiotic communication, dreamwork, reality of dreaming, marriage, death of my old man.

I will give my talk on Tuesday. On Monday I get a tryout at the house of an old man I know, attended by some people, among them Freud. I make a few false starts, but finally I get it right and say, convinced that this is true, "Everywhere where people dream they think that they are in an entirely real world." An old man to my right shakes his head vehemently. "That is not true," he exclaims. "I don't agree either," Freud adds. I am flabbergasted, realizing how true I thought this reality to be. I am flustered. People begin to leave. I sit back on my chair again. The room is now almost empty, except for Freud and some stragglers.

"Well, I must be going," Freud says.

I still want to talk to him. "So, Dr. Freud, you don't believe that the dreamworld is real?"

"No," he replies. "While dreaming you never reach the boy. And you'll always stay at a distance from the things that you are afraid of."

"That is true," I say, "but that doesn't make it less real."

"Well," Freud responds, "that's not the case. You're wrong." This old man Freud, who doesn't look like Sigmund Freud—his face is much rounder—speaks with certainty. He wipes my argument away with absolute authority.

I say, almost desperate, that everywhere in the world where I've discussed dreams, people always considered the dream environment real while dreaming.

"Well," he concludes, "research the dream reports of one hundred and one dreamers and you'll see that it is not true." Then he leaves. I sit in my chair, totally stunned. I want to write a letter to Freud to get back to this discussion. But I know that he is long dead. That I can't write an old letter. I know that I am in two worlds. Then I realize that if I send it to the Berggasse in Vienna, Freud's home address, it will obviously be a new letter and it won't get anywhere because Freud lived long ago. I am sad that I won't be able to reach Freud to continue the discussion.

My most fundamental idea in this book must be that the dreamworld is utterly real while dreaming, since this is the certainty attacked by Old Man Freud. Old Man Freud's round face does not look like Sigmund Freud. My face is round.

Old Man Freud is my father of fathers—the founder of psychoanalysis and practical dreamwork, who authored *The Interpretation of Dreams* when his own father died. This father of olden days in the old man's home protests my central conviction, reminding me that mine is but one of many possible points of view. Old Man Freud's certainty is the counterpoint to my own. His conviction is as strong as mine. According to his conviction real psychological matter is in the boy, in infantile conflicts, and the entire resistance system is geared to lead us away from a fundamental awareness concerning this reality of childhood. It is either the traumas we experienced in childhood or the imaginings we had about our parents that cause us to be who we are. This is psychology 101—Old Man Freud psychology 101.

I apparently agree with Old Man Freud that dreams can lead one away from the meat of the matter, moving us away from where it hurts within ourselves. Resistances can easily keep us floating on the surface of the dream. Mercury, god of dreaming, is known to be deceptive. However, dreamwork demonstrates how you can get down to the essence of reality by taking the dreamworld as entirely real. Dreamwork can lead to a transformative confrontation with reality. To the rational, developmentally oriented O. M. Freud of *my* dream, childhood is the true source of neurosis: depth, therefore, can only be discovered in the nursery.

As I observe for a while what passes between O. M. Freud and Robbie, I notice that it is a discussion between a younger and an older man. The younger man sounds defensive. He has to carry his own reality, different from that of the old man.

I stand before a new world, a double world where several realities, like life and death, exist simultaneously. And I live in an era different from that of my old man.

●   ●   ●

There is one last, short dream. Then the drama stops unfolding. This last dream (53) is like a period at the end of a story, a conclusion to this change of season from early to mature adulthood. After this I don't remember another dream for a long time.

I'm sitting with my father and Deanne, my wife, and I say that I'm so terribly afraid of death. I'm crying. Pappie comes over to me and is very kind. He agrees how important it is to realize my fear and to cry. In the presence of my wife— witness to my entire adult life until death do us part—I feel deeply comforted as I'm being consoled by my dead father.

Appendix

Dream Material Processed in Chapter Eight

Sydney

(1)   At party. A woman friend sits at long table. I kiss her. My wife, Deanne, is there. She looks gray and old. My friend tells me that she hasn't told me the whole story. She has already filed papers for divorce. Then she sits at other table. I get up alone and go home and watch a silly erotic flick. The kids are home and will watch a film in living room that a young girl has brought. I am bored.

(2)   At the wedding of the daughter of a friend of mine in Holland. It takes place at the Binnenhof (Inner Court). The queen of the Netherlands is there. I enter through a hall. Since the queen is there, I'm being checked at a long table. I say that my name is Bosnak. John Bosnak, my elder brother, is already there. "Just go in," the woman says. There is a double wedding. On the podium there are two brides. To the right is the queen in a pew all by herself. I am in a wooden pew some eight rows down. The other bride is talking to the audience. Her younger brother comes up and wants to say something. A struggle ensues. Then we are in the back yard. The queen is there and

comes over to me. I tell her that I am one of her subjects abroad. She says: "Ah, you want to be in a little class." I see that she is right, that I have trouble being alone as a Dutchman. That this is what I have to learn. She introduces herself as the wife of a famous Dutch novelist. Now she is gray and not the queen.

(3)   At a conference of a famous older teacher, right after a conference of my own. He gets everyone in ecstasy. Someone tells me I look exhausted. All the books around me are written by others. I feel ineffective.

(4)   In bed with young woman who wants oral sex with me. First I let her, then I stop her. I say that it is not possible. We both want it but we have to stop.

(5)   Cable TV will be all over the world. We are building a privacy wall on top of the roof so we can use it for sunbathing. A young Dutch woman friend is there. In the home of a powerful woman who was like an evil stepmother to me. Frightening mystery. Suddenly this "stepmother" is gone. There is a message on the answering machine. Then I go to a roof terrace where I see the stepmother and her daughter. They are both much younger. Stepmother is fifty, her daughter thirty. They look very pasty and frightening. I know that they are ghosts. I scream. They come up to me dressed in red. I don't believe that they are real, but they frighten the hell out of me. I touch the stepmother and my hand goes right through.

(6)   A ghost-man stands by a red door leading to another world.

(7)   In a twilight zone. Man loves woman who loves him. But they are not in this world. Each of them is loved by one of the other sex in this world. They will pass through to this world by way of the love their earthly lovers feel for them. In this way they can become real and be together. They will use the love of the others. Then they reach each other and she says, "Where are we?" He answers, "We are in a place that doesn't exist!" Then there is an explosion.

(8)   Somewhere with my Viennese psychiatrist friend in a living room with the dining table of my childhood home. While he is giving us food he is looking across at a concrete building. It looks almost like a parking garage. He has just realized that the publisher he has been looking for is right across the street from him and has always been there.

Melbourne

(9)   Dress designer friend of my old, close friend Annie shows beautiful dresses on a streetcar show. They're gorgeous. She isn't the least bit interested in me.

I was pissing out dreadful animals. I am standing in a shower with beautiful wood. We are in Melbourne. First it looks like mucus. Then I see that there is a worm in it that looks like a fresh, sweet shrimp (amaebi sashimi). Then there is an insect with wings, long legs, and antennae with the slimy consistency of a snail covered in gelatin. White. Then there are many of them. I see that my penis has torn at the head to let them pass. Deanne comes in with her father. They say that nothing is the matter. I have to go to the hospital. Her father says he hopes I will share a room with an uncle who died of a stroke (but now he was still alive). There is one single bed.

(10)   Some woman friend brings up her kids with beating and fear. They vomit. "Downstairs" neighbor-love of a wealthy man whose two sons are playing pool upstairs and watching a movie about us. I told the woman she is much too rough.

In the Outback

(11)   Boat wants to leave. I go to the White House and enter the Oval Office through a large door. Am pleased to be here and that I am so familiar with the place. I see President Clinton, who is very insecure. He is glad I'm there and takes me to a meeting of the Cabinet. I only recognize one friend from Washington. The meeting is next to a dark, rectangular pit. Suddenly, prehistoric birds fly up. They are red with gigantic, glowing red wings. I ask my friend if these are pterodactyls. He says no. They are archaic birds I have never seen. Then it is five years later. A new communication system has been developed that uses very elegant feminine units which give universal access.

(12)   "You are being treated with more respect than others [like him]," the man is told. Behind a blue car going very quickly down the tunnel near my childhood home.

Part of this dream discussed with Ilyatjari and Nganyinytja:
(13)   A room with double doors sliding. In the doorway in the Dutch house my father's elder brother is standing, dressed as a bon vivant. He has a fight with Mammie, my mother. I take his side. I forget what the fight is about. I

see my uncle with a foulard draped around his neck and a checkered suit possibly with knickerbockers, as if he were dressed for the Mardi Gras he used to love so much. I storm out. At the door I see Pappie, my father, sitting on a couch. I look at him and decide that I haven't seen him for so long, I'd better stay. He had been very ill and had almost died, but he hadn't. I go over to the couch, which is at the opposite side of the door. I hug him and tell him how much I love him.

After having been shown the Ngintaka trail and hearing Diana, our anthropologist guide and translator, speak about the woman who had become sick, nauseous, from the vomiting trail:
(14)   I am with a group wanting to understand the dreaming. There seems to be an old group and a new group. I join the old group and become terribly nauseous. I remember the vomiting dreaming of the Ngintaka. Also the vomiting dance. When I wake up I see the clouds above me. A gigantic eagle with a wingspan crossing the sky flies overhead. After a few seconds of observation it disappears. Then there is a flash of lightning and it begins to drizzle. I get up to cover our belongings.

(15)   I am tired and want to take a nap for lunch. Old Ethan is there and he is very ill. I see him on the train. There is no medicine for him. A woman in the train will help. I want sweets, can't find any. Want marzipan. Then in a Swiss *konditorei* (bakery) near the Springhouse stop (where I had my first analytical practice). Woman is young and shows me the goods. Then I go on to give a lecture. A very interesting man in a wheelchair comes up to me to ask me about things. There are other people coming up all the time and I can't get to him. Finally I have a chance. I

cross the hall to go to him. It is a light hall (like the one where I had attended a lecture by Laurence van der Post for the yearly Jung memorial, when I told everyone I was not going to stay in Switzerland but would move to the United States). As I walk up to him, one of the loves of my youth comes in. I'm very happy to see her, but I also want to get to the man. She faints and finally dances me out the door. I am sorry that I don't get to see the man.

Back in Alice Springs

(16) I am in a very ordinary room. I know that there is a room behind it. But the fear begins to come up. It overwhelms me and I begin to scream. I have had this fear before but never in such an ordinary room.

We have been taken to a lower place on a dreaming track. The dorsal fin of a land shark is following Deanne. Very scary.

A longtime student of mine is very upset about the changes in the way I work. "Everyone can do with their work as they please," I say. Then we have dinner. I sit with a very attractive woman. Have to tell her that I'm married. She is very disappointed.

Adelaide

(17) I'm at a conference. We are sitting at long tables. I am sitting with two women analyst-trainees of mine. One says that she has not been to my lecture but has listened to an old tape of mine. It had been on "the Shadow." The other has not been to my lecture at all. I am disappointed that no one has been to my lectures. I go out. I shuffle past the rows of people. Then James Hillman, one of my training analysts, is talking. It is apparently in his honor. And everyone is yelling James, James, James, James, James. It is

his conference. I am jealous of him because he is so productive. Of course people want him. I don't feel I write
anything. I haven't produced very much. Then I am sitting
in Adelaide with an organizer of my practicum there. She
has set out my lectures in detailed points. They are about
the Eleusinian mysteries, the women's mysteries. Each moment of the movement is there, like a prewritten sym-
phony. But it is not my talk. But that is what she expects
me to talk about. I will talk about the Eleusinian mysteries.
I don't have it so detailed in my mind as she has it on
paper. She has it point by point in carbon copy. I go out
the door and walk down the street. A street with a sidewalk. I want to have the program of my lecture to see
what I have promised. I go out to get it. I am in a bookstore where I find my publisher's catalog. It is a thick
booklet and has many photographs of me outdoors in it.
At first it looks as if they have published many of my
lectures. I am happy that so much of mine is in print.
Then I see that the book is called *The Life Outdoors.* Pictures
of me. The photographs are very rugged. I look very trim
and healthy. I don't have a double chin. They are in bright
color. I take the book back with me. I'm walking with a
woman and say to her that I couldn't be lecturing from
that script, the way this woman wants me to do. I have to
do my own. It may not be as well organized as hers, but it
is mine. She agrees. Then I come to a room where a man
and a woman are dancing. He has no voice but he knows
that if he keeps on dancing with her it will eventually
return. He knows that his love for her will eventually
bring him the voice. She is young. There is a Disney kind
of feeling to it. She looks like a Disney version of the little
mermaid. Finally they whirl into the other room where the
piano is and keep on dancing. When they have concluded

their time, he has his voice back. He sings in a loud, clear, and beautiful voice, "We now have the strangest love, the strangest love, the strangest love; we now have the strangest love, the strangest love, the strangest love; we now . . ." And they are whirling about and they are very happy, intensely happy.

(18) I am at an intersection. I take a left turn but have to go back and return. Then I am at a place en route to Boston. I take a left turn and there I come up to a crossing where each street is one way the wrong way, so I can't continue. At my right there is a gray-haired woman, a depressed patient I saw in a mental hospital for a while. She is on a bicycle as I am trying to turn to go back. I bump into her slightly and she becomes completely hysterical the way she'd be on the ward. She shrieks, "To think that you believed that you would get a Nobel Peace prize!" "I never thought that; you always said that," I reply. She is now my mother, very irritated. My reply shuts her up because it is true. "But where do you have to go?" I ask. We are on the side of the divided parkway where I'm traveling back home. "I have to go to the bar mitzvah of Robbie." She means the other boy who was called Robbie in my childhood. I ask her where. She tells me. "So maybe you can go straight, but it is a long, long bicycle ride." She says, in an irritated voice, "Just let me be!" It sounds like my mother in the dream with my father's bon vivant brother, annoyed and martyrish. She becomes my depressed patient again. She is with a friend, an older woman who is trying to calm her down. I'm in the car with someone; it seems to be one of my children. The passenger asks, "Is she crazy?" I say, "Yes."

Sydney

(19)   We are in a futuristic place with interesting machines that have their own ideas. A woman is there to thank me for coming. And to say how much she got out of it. It has to do with the return, with going back over an enormous distance. We're meeting with this man who is tall and bulky, balding with red curly hair. He says, "Sure we've met before. I know you." "Oh, yeah, I can recognize you somehow," I reply. "You're vaguely familiar." He says, "Yes, you have the other part of John (colleague)." I say, "No," but I remember being at the funeral. John has been cremated and the ashes were split and this man took one part and I the other. He said: "Yes, when you went to the bush you brought the ashes with you." We're standing in some kind of kitchen and Deanne has introduced us.

(20)   A man will see to it that I will get the day off and he will take care of the woman I am with so I can get some rest and the woman will get some rest. We're both very happy about that. People say, "Oh, my God, you do so many things." I say, "Yeah. But Sunday I'll be sleeping." We're sitting on a porch or a verandah, talking together. We're all young students.

(21)   In the middle of the night I wake up from a dream where there is black earth, black sand, and I have a pain in my chest.

(22)   I'm with a group of people. Someone is conducting the way Australia is going. We're in some kind of in a tent formation and suddenly we're going very, very fast. There has been an election and the people are very clear that this leader is not going to win the elections. The more

staid forces will win the elections. We're going very, very fast and we're running into a wall and then we break through it; we fly through and everything is in motion again—which has been his objective. He is a wild, youthful Australian. He supports Macquarie's idea about the Academy, which is in constant revolution, constant motion. [The only Macquarie I have heard of was one of the first governors of New South Wales. I have no idea about his thoughts.] It just is totally moving and breaking through. The pilot loves it because that's what he wants and that's the way the world is. It breaks through, flies off, and is entirely new.

(23) I'm going into the outback. There is a group. It is known that the most important experiences are in the dark, in the unknown. Then there is someone who heads up another group and he just breaks into the unknown a world of constant change. Ruthless. In the beginning I think it is all wrong. Not good. But later it appears that they respect that. That he has found his way through. And that they want something from the concentration of the other world to deal with themselves.

(24) There is an unknown planet we are exploring. We adapt to a dusty red circle that rolls through the red-dust landscape, but we can't really do it.

(25) I'm being sued for malpractice because of sexual misconduct. All accusations have been disproven. We are in Leiden, my alma mater. There are students who come to my aid and there especially is one young man who is coming to my door. At first I have seen him standing near the canal along the Academy building. He stands outside

and I let him in. Then others enter as well. One is an extremely brilliant one I trained with whom I envied. A young woman from law school says, "The time you didn't work is lost. You will not be reimbursed. But there will not be a criminal or civil suit. The case is probably going to be thrown out."

Los Angeles
(26)   It is a large room. There are pictures around on the walls like a real student room from my Leiden days.

(27)   At a conference where we're talking about Pitjantjatjara. It is a Jungian conference and all the experts on Australia are very upset because we shouldn't be talking about this. It should be kept in the area of the experts. Someone says that we should try to understand the individuals. I say, "No, it is important to first feel the foreignness of the whole culture. Only then can we begin to understand and feel the individual." I feel there is an artificial split between the individual and the culture. One of the experts comes in. A young man, like a serious student. He says, "We've done all these studies and now you are all doing this. In the end you'll end up walking behind."

Home
(28)   There is a demonstration going on across the street from my home. At first I think it has to do with existentialism, xenophobia, and the treatment of foreigners. But it is something commercial. Not genuine. Something like Benetton. United Colors. A lot of people end up in our kitchen and I have to ask them to leave because I want to spend some time with my daughter, who is home from college.

(29)   There are nude women in my brother John's room in my childhood home to watch a movie. Someone is lying on the couch and the women all begin to undress. I get very excited and then before I reach orgasm they are finished. I want them to change once more. And one changes half. A friend of John's asks, "What will you be?" (in the sense of when you grow up). "But I *am* already," I respond. "But what will you *be*," he repeats. I tell him I have a solid analytical practice in Cambridge, where people come from all over to see me. An Australian colleague who is listening supports me. He says, "Many people are out of work but he has work."

(30)   I am in the mountains. Skiing in the red sand. The morning program is over and a woman is trying to convince me to go trekking. I go up to woman and ask her what she wants and she says she just wants a chat. She says a slow trek is much more introspective. But I want either her or to go skiing. So I go over to the ski shop. A Japanese man is trying to rent me skis with very old bindings. I refuse and say I want skis with bindings from at least 1970. He finds the bindings. But the wind is coming up so hard that I can't go skiing anymore. I am on the trek. There was a murder to be committed and I thought that one of the brothers was doing it. But it appeared that one of the other brothers, young Ethan, was going to kill the prime minister. He was an evil man. (Ethan or the prime minister?) I get goosebumps when I see this young man, Ethan, going down the mountain. He is singing the romantic lead in *Fiddler on the Roof*. He is very excited. But he is not going to see his own baby son because he does not want to confuse him by just appearing shortly and then disappearing again.

(31)   I am in a little village and I have both my hats. The Stetson and the Akubra. I am very proud of them. They're beautiful. Then I'm in bed talking to someone. There's a three-year-old playing with paint and we can't control him. He begins to smear the paint all over the hats. I am heartbroken. It has ruined the hats. We're going to see the brother of the old woman who lives in a nearby village. On the strip. We arrive in the village. I'm told that curiosity kills the cat. So try to uninvite it. His elderly wife invites me in.

(32)   Some boys trick me. Then they break into the library to get some beer. I have to go home. One of the teachers is to leave school and we get to a place where suddenly the whole building twists and turns. There is an earthquake and everything collapses and I've got to get away on my motorbike. But there is no more gas in it. I can't get it started. And the operator asks what I did. I say I pressed all kinds of buttons and he says, "Yeah, you really messed it up. Here is your money back, 6,000, I don't want to deal with you anymore." So we go on and get to a place and put the motorbike down. I have been nasty to everyone, also to my son, who does not look like my son. Everything is collapsing and people are furious with me and are after me. Then I run with the motorbike but it still doesn't start and someone else comes from the opposite direction. A friend of my son David. David says, "Dad, this is . . . He can fix it." But it is still empty and in the end we don't get it to run.

(33)   The whole village is chasing us. It is very bitter. It feels like the same village that I ran through when I was

chased with the motorbike. We outrun the villagers and narrowly escape. They are especially angry with a woman traveling with us who has returned to her childhood home. They try to trick her but fail. Then we get to a house. Suddenly someone's mother gets a heart attack. She is a very religious woman and asks to have a Bible put on her chest. She will die at 6:37 and we sit around keeping her last wishes. In the end we begin to sing "Amazing Grace." She is very relaxed about it and feels that it is good like this. It is at a farm. She says: "They say it is like going to another room, and that's where I'm going." We wish her a good trip. Good journey. We are very sad but it is not bad. The moment before she fell into cardiac arrest I said to her daughter: "Be careful now because your mother is going to die." During her last moments she is young. Somewhere in her thirties. We are sitting in a circle. There is a long coffee table. It is a darkish kind of room. Dying is easy when they have faith.

(34) Some new persons at the dream practicum are discussing the method and they are saying that it is just as interesting to see what makes things change. Hanako, my Tokyo dream group co-leader, laughs and says: "We go from the assumption that it is possible to feel what the other character is feeling. But that is just an assumption because maybe we cannot." I listen very carefully and say, "That is a good idea, to see what makes things change." Because I am dissatisfied that we always end up in this paradox. It is always the same and we agree to try and follow how things change. I say this is a good idea because the Jungian problem is that you always end up with the paradox. It becomes boring as well.

(35)   We are on a space mission, as in 2001. We're being brought to the earliest intermediate station, the moon, and there one of the women takes me and shows me around. It is a dark place. It is probably night. We've arrived somewhere and we are in our space clothes, which are not the ones you usually see on a moonwalk. They are like overalls. They may be orange, but I'm not quite sure. It's a night landscape. Pebbles on the ground. And I say, "Oh, my God, I didn't pick my video camera." And a woman I am walking with, one of the astronauts, says: "Oh, don't worry. See all those packages?" There are a lot of packages standing there. "They must have packed it somewhere." She says, "Look, those are the only speakers! My God, they are so expensive." "They are," I say. "They must take a lot of abuse in outer space." We come to a place that is like an ongoing patio in this intermediate station on the moon. She says, as if she suddenly remembered something, "Oh, come, I'll show you the place where it all started." She takes me by the hand and runs me over to a cave. We come in the cave and I somehow know what's going to happen. Somehow I know it. The transformation happens immediately. We are waltzing. And we're clearly in the nineteenth century. We've traveled back in time but I don't realize it at the moment. Although on the other hand I do know. She has late-nineteenth-century clothes and I wear tails. The room is large. Everybody around is waltzing. I say in broken German, "Madam, I want to marry you." She answers in the same broken German with an English accent: "Yes, I also want to marry you." I know there is something strange. Then it is as if she is an actress, yet I know that we are in the nineteenth century. And *suddenly* everything changes. People at gas stations with dirty T-shirts and I remember the word Euro-pants:

floppy pants with suspenders. We're back in some kind of town in the twentieth century, somewhere in the American Midwest or Texas. It is a tremendous shock, though I know that it is happening. But still the transformation is a tremendous shock. (As I'm writing this down I have goosebumps all over. And I know that this is very important.) This is a mission that is going on having to do with working on dreams. The mission is something like in the movie 2001: A Space Odyssey. I have to keep track of this!

(36) Someone takes us up a mountain and it is very steep. It's a ski race. It goes very, very fast. I see the best young skier I know do it first. First you go down an escalator. That gives you speed. Then you're propelled onto the course and it is extremely icy. I decide not to do it. My son and daughter are there. I see somebody jump and fly in free-fall, with somebody else. They keep on falling. It is very high. I decide to walk down together with the ski instructor. We walk down the stairs and get to the bottom station. A lot of people. I want to walk back up and say good-bye. I walk back up because I still have my jacket up there. The stairs are very old and they begin to collapse and I try to go farther up and then the whole wall falls down. It's all rotten wood and it falls out to the side. I go to the person at the ticket counter and say, "The wall just fell down." He says, "All at your own risk. No refunds." I say, "No, that's not what I mean. I want to say that the wall fell down." He says, "Okay, we'll paper it up." Before this we'd had a discussion if I had to pay now that the wall fell down. I say, "No, it's an international principle of law. They should be happy that I'm not suing them. It's not my responsibility that it's all rotten." And then I see my

daughter in the long line of people that weaves through the bottom station. She is going to go up again and get my coat. Then she'll come down with it.

(37)   I'm in a barn and everything is dusty and sandy. There will be very little time. Anything that comes from there will be with very little time.

(38)   I am in my childhood home and look out the window. A young Dutch woman friend of mine is upstairs. She tells me to come up because I'll have a better view from up there. So I come up to another room on the same (top) floor. She says, "Come, come here, you'll see better." So I go into the room. It's the great love of my youth. She is just as beautiful as in the past. Her legs are covered with a blanket and I kiss her feet through the blanket.

(39)   We are in a house that has a very difficult passage. You had to wring yourself through a very narrow part near the stairwell. We are in Holland at the wedding of my best friends. I sit at the head table next to the groom's mother and across from his father. Across from me there is a black woman. First there is a needle sticking out of her skin. Then I feel a needle stick out of my skin as well. Something further sticks out under the eye. A kind of jack, of the game of jacks. Then I take a jack out of my mouth. It is one with four sides. More and more jacks come out of my mouth. It is happening to the black woman as well. In the beginning the groom's parents are amused. But then they begin to find it awful. They say, "Robbie, this is crazy, this is going too far. You can't do this. This is ridiculous. Terrible." They get up. I run away from the table and go somewhere. I see the bride. She is upstairs. Now

there are no longer jacks in my mouth. She is dressed beautifully. She is wearing a gown of old silk. It shines beautifully. It has a light ivory color. It also looks a little like taffetta. I bow to her and she laughs. She is surrounded by all of her bridesmaids. Then I find a map. A very ancient map. I am now someone else. A blond fellow student with a classical Latin surname, whose father had been an ambassador with a home on a Greek island. I/he find(s) the map. There is a drawing in it. And the drawing has a square with an X inside, an onion-shaped dome on top. The whole picture reminds me of an hourglass. He walks with this drawing through many adventures. Many things happen that he has to get through. And in the end he comes back to the wedding with the scroll under his arm—he has been able to hold on to the scroll through all his trials and tribulations. But it is all over now. He is terribly ashamed for all the mess he has made there. The long tables are empty and the chairs lean against them. It is really a feeling of after-the-great-party, which he has missed entirely. Then he goes over to the river and sits on the grass. Suddenly he sees to his left, on the riverbank, a building. The building is exactly, but exactly, the drawing he has carried with him through all these trials and adventures (as I write this down I have intense goose bumps). It reads on it in Dutch: *"Dit is het ontwerp van de wereld."* ("This is the design/blueprint of the world.") He looks at it and I stand next to him. He sees it and it is fantastic to behold. And then it immediately becomes very old. It disappears, entirely decayed, out of this world. It looks like the whole building is driving off; it goes away. I tell him: "I have enormous respect for you that you have done all this! Because it really was there. You held on to the image. Because you did it like you did, you've been able to hold on to the image. The image was really present. The building has truly existed. Nobody knows it but you. You've kept the image. You know it. And I don't believe that I'd have ever been able to do so. I already got scared when things went wrong at the table with the jacks in my mouth next to the parents. I already found that a terrifying experience." The building had been made of wood, old wood. It was a geometrical form. At first when it was new, it was very beautiful. And then it very quickly became old. Because it was all long, long ago. A certain game was played before the wedding. Someone went through a certain transformation all the time. Because suddenly I saw him sit somewhere as a dressed-up animal. Something to do with an elephant. The game had to do with the notion that everything had meaning and everything was meaningful to a ridiculous degree. I am amazed that he kept it all going. That he actually kept going so he would finally see the building. The Entwurf. It was like a mill where grain was pounded. Very ancient, very, very ancient.

(40)   Before I can tell my experiences with Aboriginals I have to let the can show. Somehow the can has something to do with cause (as in cause and effect). All along there are possibilities for entry into this space that is now in the can.

There is a man who is flying with me with his can. He is an older man.

(41)   I have a meeting with an attractive man, Jerry, who showed me the night life of a large Australian city. We were with three friends. We're in a car. A white old American clunker. My night-life guide is driving on the right side of the car. I am already telling him about being in two

worlds at the same time. He understands perfectly. We
have a very good communication. I sit in the passenger
seat on the left. The other two may be in another car. I
have things with me that I have to send back home. I'm
very surprised that I am in two places at the same time. He
and two of his friends are going to take me out to meet
with black women friends of theirs with whom we will
have sex. At first we come to a room where women are
baking. Their skin looks like bread. Or more like a soufflé
of egg white. It is very steamy, sweaty and hot. One of
the women is suddenly coming under water and her head
shrinks. Something like the wicked witch of the west in
The Wizard of Oz, but different. Not threatening. Then
there are some things I have to send back home to the
other world. We go to a post office where they ask me for
identification. My driver's license has no picture on it. I
can see the photo actually disappear as I am showing it to
the man behind the counter. They will make a photograph
and put it on the passport so I will have an identification
in this world. I say to my night guide: "This is just the
same as in other stories you hear about ghosts." Meaning
that they have no face, no reflection in the mirror. It almost looks like a temporary post office. I am in two places
at the same time. I am in America and I am here in Australia and that is impossible. He nods; he knows the problem.
He tells it to his friend in a language I do not understand.
So I have to send these things back home and have to
pack them and put them in a box. The box is on the right
side of the post office. But I cannot take the wooden box
that stands there. I have to get another box and my friends
are leaving. I do not want to miss the sex, so I say to the
post office clerk that I will leave it here and will come
back, because in this double life I can do anything without

being found out. I feel completely without responsibility. So I run after them down a hill and don't see them. It is a low building and houses are connected in a small settlement. I run around to find them. There are parties going on everywhere. Young people like on the Vineyard. It is seven in the morning. A man comes up to me who has been living in Japan for three months. I say Japan is a great country. We are in Japan. Then I see my friends again, the three men. I am very happy. I hope we will now get to the place. Then I begin to lose the reality. I try to hold on to it, but it fades. I wake up.

While I am in this other life I do an experiment. I close my eyes and imagine that I am in this other life. This experiment is very different from actually being there, because when I open my eyes, everything around me is totally real. And I feel it and I know it and I can touch it and it is completely and totally real. Yet when I imagine it with my eyes closed it is still wispy and not real. So the difference between recall and actuality remains the same in the dreamworld as it is in the physical world.

(42) I am with a man and I ask him to get in touch with my Australian night-life guide, Jerry, for me. He says that he doesn't know him. "I thought he was a friend of yours." He refuses to give me his own telephone number so that I can reach him.

(43) When two spirit beings want to inhabit the same place, when they want to come through at the same time, then they each have to have a little less of reality, because they can't both be real and both come in. So they have to

wear a little coat to lessen their reality. Otherwise they cannot be both in the same place. This is what happened. I feel as if I'm getting ngankari lessons.

(44)   A teacher will show me how things are done. But it has to be done together with the Western mind, and so it takes a long time, and when it can get really started the Westerner has to leave. Around a round table waiting for the right moment. The spirit doctor is no longer or not yet in his strength.

(45)   In Amsterdam on our way to the hotel. We (my wife, Deanne, and I with a lot of suitcases) get lost in the cellars and end up near the slums. We go back to the travel agent. He is the stocky detective in the movie *Who Framed Roger Rabbit.* He decides he will help us because it is dangerous. My best friend and I go back to get the luggage through the cellars. In the end we got back and were in the erotic night life district in Paris. Someone says, "Here you know what you get. You go after what you desire. And it is not as dangerous as getting lost in the cellars."

First Week Back at Work

(46)   Two double bookings in a row in my analytical practice. With one analysand I've done this twice in a row now. There is a bed in my office I have to fold up.

(47)   We are talking about Annie's friend who is still angry with me because I had let Annie down during the last year of her life. My mother thinks it quite reasonable that she is angry.

(48)   With my wife and daughter on a long journey by car. We come to a rest stop. We go in. In the men's room to piss. The brother of my Australian night guide, Jerry, walks in with his male lover. They are arm in arm. The lover is slim with dark hair. The brother is more dark blond. He says, "Yes, my brother has been away but he will write to you soon." I am very glad because I wanted to get back in touch with him. I don't want to use the toilet because of the gay brother and my attraction to his lover. The lover looks like a gentlemanly student friend. He asks how big my . . . is. (I can't hear word on my tape recorder. [sic!])

(49)   The other Robbie from my childhood takes me to his home on the park named after the queen who had been at the wedding in the Inner Court. We go upstairs. We are alone. I say, "Jeez, I haven't been here for ages. . . . That is not true," I correct myself. "I still saw your father here before he died." The pond behind the park is beautiful with the beautiful orange colors of a sunset. He asks if I want a drink. I ask for tonic water.

(50)   We are in a restaurant, a fast-food place. The table is of white marble on a single stainless leg. With Mammie, Pappie, and my brother John. Pappie has in fact been very ill but he seems to be recuperating and Mammie wants to start traveling again. She wants to go to Paris. I ask Pappie if it isn't all much too much for him. He says, "Yes. Well, we'll have to see." He looks worried and begins to cry because he is too tired and can't go along. "Well," I say, "then Mammie can go by herself and John will come to be with you for a weekend. And I would also love to come for a weekend." I look at his skin. I love him so much! He

cries and begins to slouch down, slipping almost under the table. I seat myself next to him. Then we are in the car. I think "Gee, I have been at his funeral. How is that possible? So he must just have been very ill." Then I realize that I must be dreaming. He is sitting to my right. John is driving but it is not John. And the only thing I know is how much I love Pappie. He is wearing his white cap.

(51)   This is about different hats. In the nineteenth century.

Bibliography
of Related Work

On Australia:

Cowan, James, *Mysteries of the Dream-Time: The Spiritual Life of Australian Aborigines.* Bridgeport, Dorset: Prism Press, 1992.

Elkin, A. P., *Aboriginal Men of High Degree: Initiation and Sorcery in the World's Oldest Traditions,* Rochester, Vt.: Inner Traditions, 1994.

Tacey, David, *Edge of the Sacred: Transformation in Australia.* Melbourne: HarperCollins, 1995.

On Dreaming:

Bulkeley, Kelly, *The Wilderness of Dreams.* Binghamton, N.Y.: State University of New York Press, 1994.

Bynum, Edward Bruce, *Families and the Interpretation of Dreams.* Binghamton, N.Y.: The Harrington Park Press, 1993.

Constable, G., ed., *Dreams and Dreaming.* New York: Time-Life Books, 1990.

Corbin, Henry, *Creative Imagination in the Sufism of Ibn-Arabi.* Princeton, N.J.: Princeton University Press, 1969.

Delaney, Gayle, *Breakthrough Dreaming: How to Tap the Power of Your 24-hour Mind.* New York: Bantam Books, 1991.

Faraday, Ann, *Dream Power.* New York: Berkeley Publishing, 1972.

Freud, Sigmund, *The Interpretation of Dreams.* New York: Avon Books, 1965.

Gackenbach, Jane, and Jane Bosveld, *Control Your Dreams.* New York: Harper & Row, 1989.

Garfield, Patricia, *Creative Dreaming.* New York: Ballantine Books, 1974.

Gendlin, Eugene T., *Let Your Body Interpret Your Dreams.* Wilmette, Ill.: Chiron Publications, 1986.

Hall, James A., *Jungian Dream Interpretation: A Handbook of Theory and Practice.* Toronto: Inner City Books, 1983.

Hartmann, Ernest, *The Nightmare: The Psychology and Biology of Terrifying Dreams.* New York: Basic Books, 1984.

Hillman, James, *The Dream and the Underworld.* New York: Harper and Row, 1979.

Hobson, J. A., *The Dreaming Brain.* New York: Basic Books, 1988.

Jung, C. G., *Dreams.* Princeton, N.J.: Princeton University Press, 1974.

Kelsey, Morton, *Dreams: A Way to Listen to God.* Mahwah, N.J.: Paulist Press, 1978.

Krippner, Stanley, ed., *Dreamtime & Dreamwork.* Los Angeles: Jeremy Tarcher, 1990.

LaBerge, S. L., *Lucid Dreaming.* Los Angeles: Jeremy Tarcher, 1985.

Mack, John, *The Nightmare.* New York: Columbia University Press, 1989.

Maguire, Jack, *Night & Day: Use the Power of Your Dreams to Transform Your Life.* New York: Fireside, 1989.

Maybruck, Patricia, *Pregnancy & Dreams.* Los Angeles: Jeremy Tarcher, 1989.

Reed, Henry, *Getting Help from Your Dreams.* Virginia Beach, Va.: Inner Vision, 1985.

Savary, Louis M., P. H. Berne, and S. K. Williams, *Dreams and Spiritual Growth: A Christian Approach to Dreamwork.* Mahwah, N.J.: Paulist Press, 1984.

Siegel, Alan B., *Dreams That Can Change Your Life.* Los Angeles: Jeremy Tarcher, 1990.

Signell, Karen A., *Wisdom of the Heart: Working with Women's Dreams.* New York: Bantam, 1990.

Taylor, Jeremy, *Where People Fly and Water Runs Uphill.* New York: Warner Books, 1992.

Ullman, Montague, and Nan Zimmerman, *Working with Dreams.* Los Angeles: Jeremy Tarcher, 1979.

Van de Castle, Robert, *Our Dreaming Mind.* New York: Ballantine Books, 1994.

von Franz, Marie Louise, *Dreams.* New York: Shambhala Publications, 1990.

Watkins, Mary, *Waking Dreams.* Dallas: Spring Publications, 1992.

Wiseman, Ann Sayre, *Nightmare Help: A Guide for Adults and Children.* Berkeley, Calif.: Ten Speed Press, 1986.

A much more comprehensive list of titles on dreaming is available through:

Association for the Study of Dreams (ASD)
P.O. Box 1600
Vienna, Virginia 22183
U.S.A.

Acknowledgments

This book owes its existence to Deanne, Learka, David, Annemie, and Arthur Bosnak.

And to John Bosnak, David Tacey, John Baber, Diana James, Nganyinytja, Ilyatjari, Rodney Cole Ravenswood, Trevor Baker, Anne Noonan, Brendon McPhilips, Susan Dwyer, Christine Zsizsmann, Dianne Sutton, Pemo Theodore, Sybe Terwee, Petra Branderhorst, Monica Linschoten, Aad van Ouwerkerk, Rudolf Ritsema, James Hillman, Henry Corbin, Aniela Jaffé, Adolf Guggenbühl-Craig, C. G. Jung, Sigmund Freud, Toni Frey-Wehrlin, Mario Jacoby, Angelyn Spignesi, W. Fred Long, Stephan Rechtschaffen, Mickey Lemle, Ling Lucas, Jean Christoph Boele van Hensbroek, Hanako Hamada, Juliana Simon, Monique, Robert Sheavly, Sarah Jackson, Roger Talbot, Greg Shaw, Maggie Bromell, Deirdre Barrett, Roseanne Armitage, Rita Dwyer, Kimberly Anthony Nichols, Dawn Werneck, Donna Clark, Barbara Fish Lee, and Françoise Gaarland-Kist, as well as to my perceptive editors Ed Vesneske, Jr., and Stephanie Gunning.

About the Author

Born after the war in the Netherlands, Robert Bosnak received his degree in law and criminology from the Leiden University Law School and continued his studies in Zurich, Switzerland, where he received his diploma in Analytical Psychology from the C. G. Jung-Institute in 1977. Since then he has been in private practice in Cambridge, Massachusetts, while teaching dreamwork worldwide. His first book, *A Little Course in Dreams*, is generally considered to be a classic on the practice of dreamwork and has been translated into a dozen languages. Robert Bosnak has also organized international conferences on depth psychological undercurrents in politics. He has been married for most of his life and is the father of two adults.